For
Prem & Arunjot
with Warm Regards

Sunil

22 Jan 93

The Autobiography of an Indian Monk

1. Shri Purohit Swami

The Autobiography of an Indian Monk

Shri Purohit Swami

with an introduction by
W.B. Yeats

and edited with an essay on the author by
Vinod Sena

Munshiram Manoharlal
Publishers Pvt Ltd

ISBN 81-215-0546-X
This edition 1992
Originally published in 1932 as "An Indian Monk, His
Life and Adventures" by Macmillan & Co. Limited, London
© 1992 Shri Purohit Swami Memorial Trust
© 1992 Vinod Sena for editorial essay,
notes, index and photographs

Published by Munshiram Manoharlal Publishers Pvt.
Ltd., Post Box 5715, 54 Rani Jhansi Road, New Delhi
110055 and printed at Gayatri Offset Press, Noida 201301.

Dedication

SALUTATION to my most Gracious Master, who led me through darkness to light!

I was full of ignorance, but He showed me the path to Wisdom. I was deeply immersed in misery, but He was so kind as to swim with me to the shore of bliss. I had been constantly among half-truths, but He took my hand and led me out of that maze. There had been a curtain between me and Him; solely by His benevolence was it drawn aside, so that I realised in full the meaning of life.

Salutation, yea, thousands of salutations, to Him for having merged me, an insignificant drop, into the ocean of His Being.

Contents

List of Illustrations
Author's Preface xi
Introduction xii
Life and Works of Shri Purohit Swami xxii

Chapter 1
How the Soil had been Prepared 1

Chapter 2
Grandmother and Nursing Mothers 4

Chapter 3
I am not to be a Landlord 6

Chapter 4
You are a Brahmin; be a Brahmin Always! 10

Chapter 5
Mahatmas and the Divine Master in a Cobra 15

Chapter 6
The Philosophy of Riches 19

Chapter 7
The Great Yogic Powers 23

Chapter 8
The Astrologer's Prediction 29

Chapter 9
The Engine Refuses to move 34

Contents

Chapter 10 — May Shri Gurudeo Bless You!	40
Chapter 11 — Come to Me	46
Chapter 12 — Practise Penance	50
Chapter 13 — God and Mammon	58
Chapter 14 — The God's Bed	62
Chapter 15 — Mysticism is not Mystery, it is Mystery Unveiled	68
Chapter 16 — Religion versus Spirituality	73
Chapter 17 — The Kundalini	78
Chapter 18 — Truth knows no Defence	81
Chapter 19 — My Master	84
Chapter 20 — Samadhi	88
Chapter 21 — The Touchstone	92
Chapter 22 — For My Sake	95
Chapter 23 — The Ordeal of Service	98
Chapter 24 — Go Back, My Child	102

Contents

Chapter 25	I know Him too Well!	105
Chapter 26	The Begging-Bowl	109
Chapter 27	I am Dattatreya	113
Chapter 28	Another Temptation	117
Chapter 29	My Lord Shrikrishna	121
Chapter 30	A New Lease of Life	125
Chapter 31	The Dream of the Himalayas	129
Chapter 32	Who showed Me the Way?	136
Chapter 33	The Mandate	140
Chapter 34	Out at Last!	144
Chapter 35	The Assassin's Dagger	147
Chapter 36	I am Brahma!	150
	Epilogue	152
	Prayer	154
	Index	155

List of Illustrations

1. Shri Purohit Swami. — frontispiece
2. Purohit Swami with W.B. Yeats at Palma, Majorca, 1936. — xvii
3. Temple at Narsoba Wadi on the banks of the Krishna. — 37
4. Hamsa Swami as a young sanyasin, photograph kept by Purohit Swami during his travels. — 42
5. The Dattatreya Peak of Mount Girnar. — 52
6. Lord Dattatreya, after Bhat's painting. This picture along with his guru's was carried by the author wherever he went. — 57
7. Parvati (Godavari) Purohit in middle age. — 72
8. Prem Nivas at Tapovan Ashram, Lawasha. — 106
9. Shiva Temple at Kedarnath. — 134

Author's Preface

Dr. W. B. YEATS said he wanted from me a "concrete life, not an abstract philosophy"; here is the result. Had it not been for him, I do not think I would ever have persuaded myself to attempt this autobiography. If any readers find enlightenment in the following pages, let them join me in thanking the greatest living Irish poet.

Mr. T. Sturge Moore gave much time and labour to the clarifying and arranging of this book, and I thank him.

Sir Francis Younghusband, whose interest in Indian affairs is well known, kindly went through the manuscript and made some very valuable suggestions. I am indebted also to Mrs. Gwyneth Foden, the novelist and journalist, whose affinity with our spiritual life Indians have recognised, for she has secured a place in their hearts as though she were one of themselves—to her I owe the title of this book; to Mr. Paul Brunton, who had gone to India in search of his soul's peace; to Mr. Durga Das of the Associated Press of India; Lady Elizabeth Pelham and Mrs. Margot Foster for their keen interest in my misson; and Mrs. Rennie Smith, who made the typed copy for me.

I thank them all.

Purohit Swami

London
15th March 1932

Introduction

I WROTE an introduction to the beautiful *Gitanjali* of Tagore, and now, twenty years afterwards, draw attention to a book that may prove of comparable importance. A little more than a year ago I met its author, but lately arrived in Europe, at Mr. Sturge Moore's house. He had been sent by his Master, or spiritual director, that he might interpret the religious life of India, but had no fixed plan. Perhaps he should publish his poems, perhaps, like Vivekananda, go to America. He had gone to Rome thinking it was but courteous to pay his respects to the Holy Father, but though the Abbots of the most orthodox Hindu shrines had given him their blessing, and "the organiser of the Bharat-Dharma Mahamandal ... a general letter of introduction", he was not received. Then he had come to England and called upon the Poet Laureate, who entertained him. He is a man of fifty, broken in health by the austerities of his religious life; he must have been a stalwart man and he is still handsome. He makes one think of some Catholic theologian who has lived in the best society, confessed people out of Henry James's novels, had some position at Court where he could engage the most absorbed attention without raising his voice, but that is only at first sight. He is something much simpler, more childlike and ancient. During lunch he and I, Sturge Moore, and an attaché from the Egyptian Legation, exceedingly well read in European literature, discussed his plans and ideas. The attaché, born into a Jewish family that had lived among Mohammedans for generations, seemed more Christian in his point of view than Moore or myself. Presently the attaché said: "Well, I suppose what matters is to do all the good one can." "By no means", said the monk. "If you have that object you may help some few people, but you will have a bankrupt soul. I must do what my Master bids, the responsibility is His." That sentence, spoken without any desire to startle, interested me the more because I had heard the like from other Indians. Once when I stayed at Wilfred Blunt's I talked to an exceedingly religious Mohammedan, kept there that he might not run himself into political trouble in India. He spoke of the coming independence of India, but declared that India would never organise. "There are only three eternal nations", he said, "India, Persia, China; Greece organised and Greece is dead." I remembered too that an able Indian doctor I met when questioning London Indians about Tagore said of a certain Indian leader. "We do not think him sincere; he taught virtues merely because he thought them necessary to India." This care for the spontaneity of the soul seems to me Asia at its finest and where it is most different from Europe, the explanation perhaps why it has confronted our moral earnestness and control of Nature with its asceticism and its courtesy.

We sat on for a couple of hours after lunch while the monk, in answer to my questions, told of his childhood, his life at the University, of spiritual forms that he had seen, of seven years' meditation in his house, of nine years' wandering with his begging-bowl. Presently I said: "The ideas of India have been expounded again and again, nor do we lack ideas of our own; discussion has been exhausted, but we lack experience. Write what you have just told us; keep out all philosophy, unless it interprets something seen or done."

I found afterwards that I had startled and shocked him, for an Indian monk who speaks of himself contradicts all tradition, but that after much examination of his conscience he came to the conclusion that those traditions were no longer binding, and that besides, as he explained to Sturge Moore, a monk, a certain stage of initiation reached, is bound by nothing but the will of his Master. He took my advice and brought his book, chapter by chapter, to Sturge Moore for correction. Sturge Moore, one of our finest critics, would say: "You have told us too much of this, or too little of that; you must make us see that temple more clearly", or he would cross something out, or alter a word, helping him to master our European sense of form.

Introduction

II

The book lies before me complete; it seems to me something I have waited for since I was seventeen years old. About that age, bored by an Irish Protestant point of view that suggested by its blank abstraction chlorate of lime, I began to question the country-people about apparitions. Some dozen years later Lady Gregory collected with my help the stories in her *Visions and Beliefs*. Again and again, she and I felt that we had got down, as it were, into some fibrous darkness, into some matrix out of which everything has come, some condition that brought together as though into a single scheme "exultations, agonies", and the apparitions seen by dogs and horses; but there was always something lacking. We came upon visionaries of whom it was impossible to say whether they were Christian or Pagan, found memories of jugglers like those of India, found fragments of a belief that associated Eternity with field and road, not with buildings; but these visionaries, memories, fragments, were eccentric, alien, shut off, as it were, under the plate glass of a museum; I had found something of what I wanted but not all, the explanatory intellect had disappeared. When Shri Purohit Swami described his journey up those seven thousand steps at Mount Girnar, that creaking bed, that sound of pattens in the little old half-forgotten temple, and fitted everything into an ancient discipline, a philosophy that satisfied the intellect, I found all I wanted.

III

Byzantine mystical theologians, Simeon, Callistus, Ignatius and many others, taught a form of prayer or mental discipline resembling his. The devotee must say continually, even though his thought be elsewhere, "Lord Jesus Christ, have mercy upon us"; a modern Russian pilgrim[1] of their school repeated those words daily twelve thousand times, "Lord Jesus Christ" as he drew in his

---

[1] The Rev. R.M. French has translated his autobiography into English and calls it *The Way of a Pilgrim*. "Of the pilgrim's identity nothing is known", he writes, "in some way his manuscript, or a copy of it, came into the hands of a monk of Mount Athos, in whose possession it was found by the Abbot of St. Michael's monastery at Kasan."

Introduction

breath, "have mercy upon us" as he breathed it out, until they had grown automatic and were repeated in his sleep; he became, as he said, not speaker but listener.[1] Shri Purohit Swami writes: "I repeated the Gayatri, the most sacred mantram, so habituated that even in my dreams I continued. When talking with others my mind went on unconsciously muttering 'We meditate on the supreme splendour of that Divine Being, may it illuminate our intellects'." The Russian pilgrim begged dry bread from door to door; a monk of Mount Athos is at this moment travelling through the world and living upon "fifty acorns a day." My Indian monk's habitual diet is milk and fruit, but his austerity at times has been greater; he writes of a certain pilgrimage: "I refused to take either milk or fruit by the way and only drank water from time to time; my friend sang the glory of the Master" (their divine Lord Dattatreya) "whenever I sat for rest under the shade of a tree, and would try to find and bring water to me."

IV

The prayers, however, are unlike, for the Russian's prayer implies original sin, that of the Indian asks for an inspired intellect; and this unlikeness is fundamental, the source perhaps of all other differences. The Russian, like most European mystics, distrusts visions though he admits their reality, seems indifferent to Nature, may perhaps dread it like St. Bernard, who passed the Italian Lakes with averted eyes. The Indian, upon the other hand, approaches God through vision, speaks continually of the beauty and terror of the great mountains, interrupts his prayer to listen to the song of birds, remembers with delight the nightingale that disturbed his meditation by alighting upon his head and singing there, recalls after many years the whiteness of a sheet, the softness of a pillow, the gold embroidery upon a shoe. These things are indeed part of the "Splendour of that Being." The first four Christian centuries shared

---

[1] The Swami comments, "Some of the yogis of India practise 'Ajapa-japa' mantram. 'Ajapa-japa' is very short and easy. They repeat 'Soham' as they draw in the breath and 'Hamsah' as they breathe it out. 'Soham Hamsah' means, 'I am that Hamsa'—the eternal self, or soul."

Introduction

his thought; Byzantine theologians that named their great church "The Holy Wisdom" sang it; so, too, did those Irish monks who made innumerable poems about bird and beast, and spread the doctrine that Christ was the most beautiful of men. Some Irish saint, whose name I have forgotten, sang "There is one among the beasts that is perfect, one among the fish, one perfect among men."

V

"And there are also many other things which Jesus did, the which, if they should be written every one, I suppose that even the world itself could not contain the books that should be written", but Christendom has based itself upon four short books and for long insisted that all must interpret them in the same way. It was at times dangerous for a painter to vary, however slightly, the position of the Nails upon the Cross. The greatest saints have had their books examined by the Holy Office, for East and West seem each other's contraries—the East so independent spiritually, so ready to submit to the conqueror; the West so independent politically, so ready to submit to its Church. The West impregnated an East full of spiritual turbulence, and that turbulence brought forth a child Western in complexion and in feature. Since the Renaissance, literature, science and the fine arts have left the Church and sought elsewhere the variety necessary to their existence; perhaps the converse impregnation has begun, the East as male. Being most impressed by arts that I have myself practised, I remember our selection for admiration of old masterpieces where "tonal values" or the sense of weight and bulk that is the particular discovery of Europe are the least apparent: some flower of Botticelli's, perhaps, that seems a separate intellectual existence. Then I think of the sensuous deliberation Spenser brought into English literature, of the magic of "Christabel" or "Kubla Khan", of the wise pedlar in the "Excursion" of Ahasuerus in "Hellas", and wisdom, magic, sensation, seem Asiatic. We have borrowed directly from the East and selected for admiration or repetition everything in our own past that is least European, as though groping backward towards our common mother.

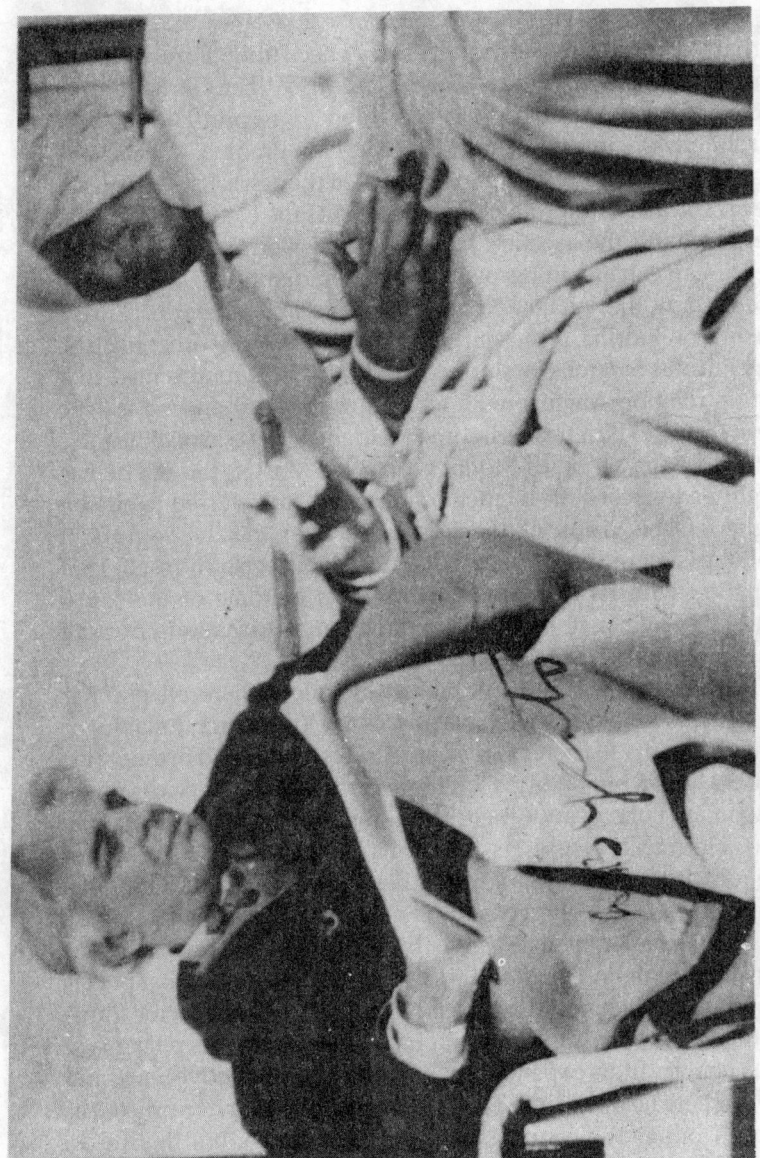

2. Purohit Swami with W.B. Yeats at Palma, Majorca, 1936

Introduction

VI

Perhaps dogmatism was the necessary check upon European violence, asceticism upon the Asiatic fecundity. When Christ said, "I and my Father are One", it is possible to interpret Him as Shri Purohit Swami interprets his Master's "I am Brahma." The One is present in all numbers, Brahma in all men though self-conscious in the ascetic alone; and the plain man admits the evidence, for, beat the pupil and the ascetic's back is scored, and the ascetic, if he please, can exhaust in his own body an epidemic that might have swept away the village. Nor can a single image, that of Christ, Krishna or Buddha, represent God to the exclusion of other images. Shri Purohit Swami worshipped God at first as represented in a certain religious picture with an exciting history and no artistic merit, come to him through some accident of his personal history, but before the ascent of Mount Girnar his Master, though he has forgotten to record the incident in this book, transferred to him by a glance "the vision of the formless"; after that he could still worship God under an image, but an image chosen by himself. That initiation with its final freedom itself an epitome of the soul's gradual escape, in its passage through many incarnations, from all that is external and predestined.

The Swami is a minstrel and story-teller where all popular literature is religious; yet all his poems are love-songs, lullabies or songs of loyalty to friend or master, for in his belief and in that of his hearers he can but offer to God the service learnt in service of man or woman; nor can any single service symbolise man's relation to God. He must be sung as the soul's husband, bride, child and friend. I asked for translations of these songs, which he sings in a sweet, not very strong voice, to a music which seems to employ intervals smaller than those of European music, especially for translations of those in Marathi, his native tongue, for what poet is at his best out of his native tongue? He has, however, sent me translations of his poems in Urdu and Hindi as well, for his pilgrimage as it encircles India expends but two months in his native State, and everywhere he must sing. The English hymn-writer, writing not as himself but as the congregation, is a rhetorician; but the Indian convention, founded upon the most poignant personal emotion,

Introduction

should make poets. The Swami has beautiful dramatic ideas, but only somebody born into one of those three tongues can say whether he has added that irrational element which has made "Sing a Song of Sixpence" immortal. This is from Marathi:

> Sweet are His eyes, sweet His looks,
> The love they look exceeding sweet,
> Sweet are His lips, sweet His kiss,
> The love displayed exceeding sweet,
> Sweet His words, His promise sweet,
> Presence and absence both are sweet,
> The pangs of love exceeding sweet.

This is from Hindi:

> I know that I am a great sinner,
> That there is no remedy,
> But let Thy will be done,
> If my Lord wishes He need not speak to me.
> All I ask is that of His bounty
> He walk by my side through my life.
> I will behave well
> Though He never embrace me—
> O Lord, Thou art my Master
> And I Thy slave.

This is from Urdu:

> Shall I do this?
> Shall I do that?
> My hands are empty,
> All that talk amounts to nothing.
> Never will I do anything,
> Never, never will I do anything;
> Having been commanded to woo Thee
> I should keep myself wide awake
> Or else sleep away my life.
> I am unfit to do the first,

Introduction

> But I can sleep with open eyes,
> And I can always pretend to laugh,
> And I can weep for the state I am in;
> But my laugh has gone for good,
> And gone the charm of tears.

And this too is from Urdu:

> A miracle indeed!
> Thou art Lord of All Power.
> I asked a little power,
> Thou gavest me a begging-bowl.[1]

VII

Our moral indignation, our uniform law, perhaps even our public spirit, may come from the Christian conviction that the soul has but one life to find or lose salvation in: the Asiatic courtesy from the conviction that there are many lives. There are Indian courtesans that meditate many hours a day awaiting without sense of sin their moment, perhaps many lives hence, to leave man for God. For the present they are efficient courtesans. Ascetics, as this book tells, have lived in their houses and received pilgrims there. Kings, princes, beggars, soldiers, courtesans and the fool by the wayside are equal to the eye of sanctity, for everybody's road is different, everybody awaits his moment.

VIII

The reader of the lives of European devotees may at first be disappointed in this book; the author's life is modelled upon no sacred example, ordered by no well-tried conventual discipline. He is pleased to remember that he learnt his book quickly at the college, that he overcame the wrestler, that he showed courage before the assassin's knife; and yet, though he display our foibles and vanities,

---

[1] Yeats included these very poems in his famous anthology, *Oxford Book of Modern Verse, 1892-1935*, pp. 223-4. *Editor.*

Introduction

he has what we have not, though we once had it—heroic ecstatic passion prolonged through years, through many vicissitudes. Certain Indian, Chinese and Japanese representations of the Buddha, and of other Divine beings, have a little round lump on the centre of the forehead; ecstatics have sometimes received, as it were from the seal of the God, a similar mark. It corresponds to the wounds made as though by nails upon the hands and feet of some Christian saint, but the symbolism differs. The wounds signify God's sacrifice for man—"Jesus Christ, have mercy upon us"—that round mark the third eye, no physical organ but the mind's direct apprehension of the truth, above all antinomies, as the mark itself is above eyes, ears, nostrils, in their duality—"splendour of that Divine Being." During our first meetings, whether within doors or without, Shri Purohit Swami's orange turban hid his forehead to the eyes, but he took it off one hot day during lunch, and I saw the little round lump. Marks somewhat resembling those made by nails have been produced upon the hands and feet of patients in a French hospital by hypnotic suggestion, and it is usual, although the wounds of the saints seen by credible witnesses were deeper, more painful, more disfiguring, to attribute those wounds to autosuggestion. My own studies, which have not been brief or superficial, compel me to admit suggestion, but to deny with a fervour like that of some humble ignorant Catholic that it can come out of the mind of the ecstatic. Some day I shall ask Shri Purohit Swami if the mark first appeared upon his forehead when he lay unconscious upon the top of Mount Girnar.

W.B. YEATS

5th September 1932

The Life and Works of Shri Purohit Swami

THE higher the ideal, the thornier the path. To conquer the "Kingdom of Heaven within" is an ideal second to none and the path to it is the one most beset with difficulties. Unless one has adamantine strength of mind, indomitable confidence in oneself, and unshaken faith in God, one cannot reach this highest goal.... Taking knowledge and perception as his able and skilful scouts, the seeker should make resolute marches onwards, under the banner of Love, with the vanguards of renunciation and perseverance, till he brings completely under his sway those blessed dominions which it is his most cherished ambition to subdue. If this be done, the Goddess of Victory shall bestow upon the warrior those high trophies which will be his eternal possession, a proud witness to his greatness and his valour.
Glory unto the warrior who has conquered "the Kingdom of Heaven within," which is his own Self [1]

The author of *An Indian Monk* is known today only to the handful of scholars who have specially studied the final phase of the literary career of his friend and collaborator, the Nobel laureate W.B. Yeats. Yet if we take even a cursory look at his life and work, we shall recognise in Purohit Swami a most distinguished son of the Indian Renaissance. He, too, was of the line of Vivekananda, Ramatirtha and Aurobindo. Having tested for himself the ancient spiritual wisdom of his country, he boldly set forth to interpret and to propagate it in opposition to western materialism and education. Indeed, he was willing to carry the battle to the very heartland of the

---

[1] Hamsa Swami, *Voice From The Himalayas*.

enemy, and spent five eventful years in London teaching yoga and publishing books on that subject. For over half a century now, readers in the West have approached our spiritual classics—*The Bhagavad Gita*, the Upanishads and Patanjali's *Yoga Sutras*—by way of Purohit Swami's flowing and uncontorted translations.[1] He served, in fact, as a vital and indispensable link between the first interpreters of Indian spirituality who went to the West at the turn of the century and the full tide of eastern mysticism which swept Europe and America during the 'sixties and' seventies.

Yet today Purohit Swami is a forgotten name in the land of his birth. He may have made a vivid impression when he went to the West during the early 'thirties, but he failed to stay there long enough to imprint himself permanently on its mind. On returning to India, he busied himself attending on his ailing guru and outlived him for barely five years. To the very last he remained a mendicant monk who founded no institution, no ashram, and accepted no disciples in his own name who could continue his work and perpetuate his memory. Even the five books which he brought out from London were never published in India—though some of them went through repeated printings in England and America.

The publication of Shri Purohit Swami's memoir in India thus acquires a rather special significance. Besides providing us with the first autobiographical account in modern times of a yogi's life and quest, it furnishes us with a fascinating record of one of the more memorable lives of modern India. It should go a long way in securing for its author the recognition which has been his due.

LIFE

In chapter 6 of *The Bhagavad Gita*, Prince Arjuna asks Srikrishna

---

[1] Faber and Faber, London, have repeatedly issued Purohit Swami's translations, in particular. *The Geeta* and *The Ten Principal Upanishads*, available in paperback since 1965 and 1970, respectively. William Gerber, in his extensive anthology, *The Mind of India* (Carbondale: Southern Illinois Un.Pr., 1967, rpt. 1977), for the Upanishads, selected the Swami-Yeats translation from among the numerous available. In 1977, Random House brought out from New York a deluxe edition of *The Bhagavad Gita* in a large format, extensively illustrated with Curt Bruce's photographs; the translation used was the Swami's.

about the fate of a disciple who, though full of faith and devotion, is unable to work out his salvation within his present life. The Lord replies:

> he who has slipped away from the path of spirituality will be born again in the family of the pure, benevolent and prosperous ....
> Then the experience acquired in his former life will revive, and with its help he will strive for perfection more eagerly than before ....
> Then, after many lives, the student of spirituality who earnestly strives, and whose sins are absolved, attains perfection and reaches the Supreme.[1]

The life of Shankar Gajannan Purohit provides a classic illustration of this text. He was born on 12th October, 1882, at Badnera in Vidarbha in the home of a pious and well-placed Brahmin family of Maharashtra. His father, Gajannan Purohit, took keen interest in his education and ensured that he was well-grounded both in traditional and modern learning. Shankar became proficient in Marathi, Sanskrit and English while still at school. He studied philosophy for his B.A. at Morris College, Nagpur, followed by Law at Deccan College, Pune, and at Bombay University. When he had completed his education and was preparing to enter life, a venerable Brahmin arrived from the south with many bundles of palm-leaf manuscripts. These, he claimed, were horoscopes derived from Sage Bhrigu, the Master Astrologer of ancient India.

The Brahmin was able to place the right horoscope for Purohit, and as he read the Sanskrit text of the predictions written out in the Malayalam script, the young man marvelled at the accuracy of its account of the family and of the first twenty-five years of his life. It spoke of spiritual experiences which he had not shared even with his family and closest friends. It went on to describe his life as a householder and subsequently as a renunciate—and time was to bear out the truth of what it said. It revealed that in his previous life Purohit had been a sanyasin, and had been reborn to complete

[1] Purohit Swami, trans., *The Geeta*, London: Faber, 1965, pp. 45-6.

within this lifetime the task of spiritual emancipation. It described him as one who would master the "Gouranda Bhasha" (that is, English) and as one who at fifty "would go throughout the world preaching the gospel of Thou art That."[1]

These predictions confirmed young Purohit in his spiritual quest and he never forgot the prophecy made about him by Sage Bhrigu centuries before his birth. The palm-leaf horoscope had indicated that his spiritual initiation would take place on Mt. Girnar. He did not have to await this for long. Natekar Swami (who later became his guru and assumed the name of Hamsa Swami) invited him for a pilgrimage to this granite hill at Junagadh sacred to Lord Dattatreya. After several days of penance and a frugal diet, the climb up the seven thousand steps leading to the third and final peak, proved extremely arduous. But it afforded Purohit his first experience of *samadhi*. Later, in a lonely temple at Mahur, he had his first physical *darshan* of Lord Dattatreya, the personal deity of his family and also of his guru.

Purohit was now faced with a paradox which has confronted many a spiritual seeker in our country—the paradox so unforgettably embodied in the life of Prince Siddhartha, the Buddha. The Indian way of life presents liberation from the wheel of birth and death as our supreme goal and parents often help to instil this into the consciousness of the child in a thousand different ways. Yet if the child responds sensitively to such teachings, and on growing up resolves to renounce ordinary living in order to pursue his spiritual quest, for the family it is as though the world itself threatens to dissolve. Seeing the direction of Purohit's inclinations, his parents sought to bind him down to the common human condition. But it was not until a holy man told Purohit that the householder's life was not a bar to spirituality and that he was destined to marry, that he gave in to parental pressure. In 1908 he was married to Godavari, or Godu Bai, who appropriately assumed the name of Parvati after the wedding. She was a woman of great understanding and fortitude, with the patience of a saint. She joined her husband in his

---

[1]Purohit Swami, "My Palm Leaf Horoscope," *Stories of Indian Mysticism*. For permission to quote from unpublished materials in the Purōhit Swami Papers (PSP), here and subsequently, I am indebted to Mrs. Mrinalini Chitale.

spiritual practices and both spent long hours in meditation and lived on a diet of milk and fruit or of milk and neem leaves. On learning of the austere life of the couple, Lokmanya Tilak is said to have come to see them. In 1910, Parvati gave birth to her first daughter, Indumati, and four years later, to the second, Sumati. When in 1915, Purohit learnt that a son had been born, he wrote to his wife for permission to renounce. Now that there was a male heir, he felt that his *pitri rin*, or debt to his forefathers, stood discharged, and Lord Dattatreya himself confirmed him in this decision through a vision. Parvati was only too aware of her husband's growing restlessness and she gave in to his plea when Dattatreya appeared to her as well in answer to her prayer for direction.

The years which followed were filled with many tests and labours. They were years of arduous meditation, great austerity and unceasing work for his guru. For a time Purohit served as manager and all-jobs-man at a candle factory owned by a disciple of Hamsa Swami. When the Swami acquired a fertile 150 acres farm at Lawasha, a few miles from the Portuguese territory of Daman, Purohit helped in various ways in the building and furnishing of the spacious main building called Prem Nivas. When the ashram had been built, Hamsa Swami directed Purohit to proceed on a pilgrimage "to Mt. Girnar", "to the four great monasteries" founded by Shankaracharya, the "seven puris," the "twelve shrines of Lord Shiva, the four of the Goddess Jagadamba, and all those dedicated to Lord Dattatreya."

Purohit Swami's travels across the length and breadth of India took up the better part of nine years. During this time he was permitted to beg only for food and that once a day. If his room was unlit, he could not ask for a candle; if down with high fever, he could not beg for medicine; if the food offered to him was too stale even for cattle he was obliged to accept it and to bless those who served it. These years of wandering as a mendicant sanyasin gave to Purohit Swami a profound firsthand experience of the complex, living tradition of Indian spirituality. But the price he paid for such knowledge was prohibitive. By the time he returned, his bodily health was shattered. He had "uric-acid trouble," "Spleen and liver refused to work, the heart was very weak, hydrocele with symptoms of sarcoma" made it impossible for him to walk. He underwent surgery in a Bombay hospital and it was months before he was quite recovered. But he was not destined to rest for long, and his dream of a life of solitude and of quiet meditation in the Himalayas was to remain a dream. Hamsa Swami told him that all that he had done so far was a preparation for his life's work and that he had to proceed to England to "interpret the esoteric phase of Indian life to the West."

Purohit Swami set sail from Bombay on the morning of 16th November, 1930. He disembarked at Venice on 1st December, and proceeded to Rome to pay his respects to the Pope. But though armed with credentials from the heads of the oldest of Hindu *maths* and monasteries, he could not obtain an audience at the Vatican. The days of ecumenism were still far away and an introduction from a European prince or potentate would have stood the Swami in better stead. After a visit to Paris, he arrived in London on the last day of February in 1931 to embark on one of the most productive periods of his life. For a time he considered proceeding to California in the footsteps of Swami Vivekananda but in early 1932 decided to stay on in England. That year he delivered a series of lectures on Patanjali, and in 1933 a similar series on Karma Yoga. He lived in a back room in an inexpensive lodging house in London, subsisted on a diet of milk and fruit, walked or rode on buses, and in all things served as a model of simple living. He was readily available for private consultations and interacted well with people from all classes and from different walks of life. In fact, he commanded the respect and loyalty of those who came in contact with him and drew many distinguished men and women to his circle, chief among them the famous Irish poet W.B. Yeats and Lady Elizabeth Pelham and her family. In course of time he founded the London Institute of Indian Mysticism with the Hon'ble L.S. Bristowe as president and Miss Vera Turner as secretary. The Institute organised lectures on Thursday evenings at 51 Lancaster Gate, W2, and was able to attract the most qualified Indian and English specialists for the purpose.

W.B. Yeats has described graphically in his introduction how he first met Purohit Swami at the home of his friend Thomas Sturge Moore. The two guests took to each other readily and the friendship which developed from this meeting proved an enduring one. The introduction to Yeats, then at the height of his fame and influence, provided the Swami an ideal point of entry into the highly-competitive and exclusive literary world of London. He was equal to the opportunity, and during the five years that he was abroad was able to place as many books with publishers there. *An Indian Monk* (1932) and a translation of Hamsa Swami's travelogue, *The Holy Mountain* (1934), were undertaken directly at Yeats's instance. These were followed by translations of our three mystical classics: *The Geeta* (1935), *The Ten Principal Upanishads* (1937) and Patanjali's *Aphorisms of Yoga* (1938). It was on Yeats's personal initiative that the books were placed with two of London's most prestigious publishers, Macmillan and Faber; and he found time to correct his friend's manuscripts and to write introductions for four of his five books. The Swami was able to cap the European phase of his work by persuading the ailing Irish poet to join him in Majorca where they collaborated on the translation of the Upanishads. When the task was complete, Purohit Swami bid the Yeatses and the West goodbye, and set sail for Bombay on 13th May, 1936.

The months which followed were spent in attending on Hamsa Swami, news of whose illness had hurried Purohit Swami home. When Yeats expressed a desire to visit India, both master and disciple extended to him a pressing invitation to come. Purohit Swami persuaded a number of leading Indian universities to sponsor a lecture-tour for the Nobel Laureate, but the plan had to be dropped on account of Yeats's declining health. On 9th June, 1937, came the blow which for the devoted disciple is the cruellest that life can bring: the final parting from one's master. From their first meeting in a flat in Bombay, Purohit Swami had loved and adored Hamsa Swami as he adored and loved no other person. He had served his guru with exemplary devotion even to the neglect of his wife and children. When at death's door abroad, Hamsa Swami had saved him by giving his *darshan*. Even though he had become one in spirit with his master, with Hamsa Swami's death it was as though his refuge, his anchor had been taken away from him. As T.S. Eliot said of Christ's disciples after the crucifixion in *The Waste Land*.

> He who was living is now dead
> We who were living are now dying
> With a little patience.

The Life and Works of Shri Purohit Swami

Such was the degree of Purohit Swami's renunciation that though he was Hamsa Swami's most distinguished disciple, he showed no desire to assume his guru's mantle and left the ashram at Lawasha never to return.

The publication of *The Ten Principal Upanishads* in 1937 had helped to make Purohit Swami's name known in academic circles. He began receiving invitations from various universities and delighted to lecture to young audiences, encouraging them not to be taken in by western materialism and to study their country's ancient spiritual wisdom. He also kept up with his literary work. In May 1937, T.S. Eliot wrote to accept *Aphorisms of Yoga* for Faber and the book was published in the following year. Purohit Swami also kept up a regular correspondence with Yeats, the last of whose letters, dated 22nd December, 1938, arrived in the New Year. The news of Yeats's death on 28th January was yet one further blow. The last years were spent on polishing the Swami's English renderings of the literature of Lord Dattatreya, in particular the *Avadhoota Gita* and the dialogues and stories associated with him. But even though they represent Purohit Swami at his best as translator, these translations were not destined to be published in the Swami's lifetime. He had suffered from serious urinary problems following his nine-years pilgrimage. These now recurred, and on his own insistence he underwent surgery in Bombay which was to prove fatal. In 1979 the translation of the *Avadhoota Gita* was published from Delhi with a scholarly introduction by Professor S. Mokashi-Punekar. Six years later, on 14th October, 1985, the Purohit Swami Papers became part of a national collection when they were gifted by the Swami's family to the Nehru Memorial Museum & Library.

The Present Work

The fateful meeting with W.B. Yeats at the London home of the poet and art-critic Thomas Sturge Moore, which led to the writing of *An Indian Monk*, took place on 6th June, 1931. For Purohit Swami it represented "the best time that I ever spent in Europe."[1] In his quest for realising "I am Brahma", the yogi renounces his worldly

---

[1] Letter to Sturge Moore of 9th June, 1931.

self, and the Swami was at first shocked by Yeats's suggestion that he write his memoirs. But he saw the force of the argument that the west was already familiar with India's mystical classics and with modern interpretations of the Vedantic philosophy. Accordingly, if Yeats "wanted my own experience, wanted 'a concrete life not an abstract philosophy',"[1] the Swami shed his initial hesitation and set about the task in right earnest. After all, a yogi who had achieved liberation was not bound by convention, and Bahina Bai, the famous seventeenth century woman saint of Maharashtra, had left behind a record of her last thirteen incarnations.

As the Swami was only newly come to England, his words lacked the force of living speech. He turned to Sturge Moore for assistance, and his friend helped make his language more idiomatic and encouraged him to dispense with irrelevant details and with abstruse discussions of Indian life and philosophy. As the work progressed, Sturge Moore came to see himself increasingly as a collaborator rather than as an editorial adviser. When instead of a share in the royalties, the Swami offered a fee, Sturge Moore took offence and totally dissociated himself from the venture.

Yeats's enthusiasm for Purohit Swami's autobiography, however, never slackened. The more he saw of its manuscript the more he liked it. After all, as Sturge Moore noted, "it was exactly the kind of book he wanted to read."[2] Having read all but the final chapters, he wrote to the Swami, "It is a form of experience of which we have had previously no record, and it is described with admirable simplicity." On completing his reading he declared, "The book is exceedingly beautiful as well as entirely unique."[3] The Swami completed his memoir by mid-March 1932, and the same month Yeats agreed to write its introduction. He met the Swami in London on 7th April, and promptly recommended the work to his own publisher. Harold Macmillan (later prime minister of the U.K.) was quick to accept the offer and wrote to Yeats, "I am very much obliged to you for bringing us this book, and I shall take the matter up at once."[4] He was as good as his word. The book was already in

---

[1] Book II, p. 1 of untitled typescript, PSP.
[2] Letter to Purohit Swami of 14th March, 1932.
[3] Yeats's letters to the Swami of 29th March and 1st August, 1932.
[4] Letter dated 15th April, 1932.

proof by June and was released in the autumn after some delay on account of Yeats's introduction.

An Indian Monk: His Life And Adventures was quick to be noticed. With so many distinguished names associated with it—W.B. Yeats, T. Sturge Moore and the diplomat-orientalist Sir Francis Younghusband—how could it have been otherwise? As one reviewer noted, "without such helpful counsel and powerful support I doubt if [the author] would have been able to prepare so sincere and striking an account of an Indian mystic's life, or to find a publisher for it when written."[1] The critical notices were generous and dwelt in particular on the simplicity, charm and sincerity of the author and on the uniqueness of the ground which he covered. Western readers could find many accounts of the lives of Christian monks living in medieval monasteries. "But very seldom indeed can one hope to find a Hindu yogi writing his own autobiography. If for nothing else, therefore, this autobiography of an Indian monk should be attractive as it conducts us through the mental conflicts, reveals the austerities, the penances, and the reactions that are experienced by the yogi." The miracle stories of sadhus and mahatmas, and the varied and at-times hair-raising adventures of the author did not go unnoticed. One critic found the work a spiritual classic and placed it among "the most illuminating messages that ever came from the pen of a profound thinker and seeker after the Truth." For her *An Indian Monk* was an eastern counterpart to *Pilgrim's Progress*:

Never since Bunyan wrote his *Pilgrim's Progress* have we had anything given to us like *An Indian Monk*. It will only be just if this book, which has surely been inspired, meets with the same universal appreciation and study as did the English tinker's revelation of a soul's quest for God.

When Yeats wrote his introduction for Purohit Swami's book, he expected it to repeat the success story of Tagore's *Gitanjali* which he had helped to launch two decades earlier. But that expectation was not to be fulfilled. For all the good notices which the volume

---

[1] The three English reviews from which I quote successively are by F. Yeats-Brown, Gwyneth Foden and N.A.L. (Reviews file, PSP).

received, it sold slowly. When the Swami's next book, *The Holy Mountain*, was ready, Macmillan turned it down even though, on their own admission, "the book seems one which deserves publication."[1] But Yeats saw no reason to revise his estimate of Purohit Swami's work and its unique significance. He tried to reassure his Indian friend by pointing out, "It is a slow business making a reputation for anything new." He cited his own experience, saying: "It was three years before I had sold more than about 60 copies of my first book ... and yet I had an enthusiastic welcome from reviewers."[2]

In approaching *An Indian Monk* we need to remind ourselves of the specific purpose for which it was written. We must not see it as a definitive record of its author's life and work. It covers only those aspects of Purohit Swami's experience which were relevant to his vocation as a yogi. In chapter 16 he observes, "There were three irons in my fire: public service, family service and service of God." He could have spoken of four since he was a gifted writer in his mother tongue and at one time had strong literary ambitions. In fact those who knew of this expected him to win international recognition one day in the manner of Tagore. *An Indian Monk* only tells us as much about the Swami's family—his grandmother, his parents and his wife—as is essential for understanding his spiritual development. It mentions four sisters, a brother and three children, but of them it says nothing. We hardly get to see the author as a householder, as husband and father, or as a friend. Nor does the memoir touch on Purohit's intense involvement with our national movement. He was a fiery revolutionary in his day and was an active lieutenant of Lokmanya Tilak until his arrest and trial. He publicly spoke in Tilak's defence, and such was the tenor of his speeches that when they were published, the pamphlet was promptly proscribed and all copies seized and destroyed.

Given such powerful competing interests, Purohit must have faced a prolonged inner conflict before opting for the spiritual life. Even if he is silent on his political commitment, he shares with us the reasoning by which he came to give it up: "I thought, yes, the

---

[1] Quoted in Yeats's letter to the Swami of 12th May, 1933.
[2] Letters dated 12th May and 24th October, 1933.

world has been created by Him, and He alone is able to help it. Then what business have I to meddle unless He bids me. My first duty is to know Him and attain direct communication with Him. In short, I thought, I should have His *adesha,* or mandate, before I did anything for this world." Through similar logic, no doubt, Purohit had put aside his literary ambitions even earlier. Like the Jesuit poet, Gerard Manley Hopkins, he eschewed all writing as a distraction from his spiritual quest. A suggestion from his spiritual superior persuaded Hopkins to take up his pen again to celebrate God's grandeur after a seven-year silence. It needed three successive visions of Lord Dattatreya and the unequivocal *adesha,* "Write for My sake," to make Purohit renounce his vow of literary abstinence. But for this mandate *An Indian Monk* and the books which followed might never have been written.

While Purohit Swami was still in England he was keen to see his books reprinted in India.[1] It seems a pity that the first of these, his autobiography, should be issued in India after almost six decades of its publication from London.[2] But if you accept the Indian point of view, nothing is by accident. Howsoever late, this edition of *An Indian Monk* is timely. It speaks of a phase of life which, under the conditions of modern social and economic change, is fast becoming *passe* in our country. For centuries we have sustained traditions which enabled sanyasins and renunciates to pursue their spiritual life without thought of their material upkeep. But with the increasing disintegration of strong local communities and of the extended family; with rapid urbanisation accompanied by unprecedented inflation; the multiplication of material needs to sustain a capitalist market economy; it is no longer possible for the ordinary householder to feed those who come to his door. The world of sadhus and fakirs, of miracle-workers who can walk on fire, stop a locomotive or step forth from a sealed room without breaking lock or door, is one in which many of us grew up, but it is a world fast disappearing for our children. *An Indian Monk* provides a memorable record of

---

[1] When negotiating the contracts for the Upanishads and Patanjali, Yeats under pressure from Purohit Swami, got Faber to agree to an Indian edition if they failed to bring out an inexpensive reprint.

[2] In 1987, a Marathi rendering of the book by Mrs. Mrinalini Chitale was published from Bombay under the title, *Mi Ek Sanyasi* (reprinted, 1989).

this world and explains and interprets to us its philosophy. In addressing the western reader, the author stops from time to time to describe the more distinctive of our social institutions. Thus of the Hindu family he says: "All relationship should, as we think, be governed by a voluntary order ... to prevent affection becoming selfish and exclusive." Thus when the son gets married, the mother "yields up her keys and authority to her son's wife, who in turn would not think of acting without having consulted her husband's mother." Again when "two married brothers live in the father's house, the children of the elder will be taught always to ask their uncle, the younger, to satisfy their material wants; to him they go for toys and sweets, etc., and vice versa." It is by such means that in an extended family children are prevented from being spoilt by parents and encouraged to look up to and love all their elders.

In countering the charge, preferred by some westerners, that our mendicant sadhus and holy men imposed an unwarranted burden on society, Purohit Swami gives a spirited account of the widespread spiritual benefits which we had reaped from such an institution. The "fee or tax" borne by the householder "was voluntary and the benefit received at once in the shape of theory or exhortation or narrative. The results of the highest development of the human faculties" were, by such a process "in the most human and gracious manner diffused equally through all classes in proportion to the individual's readiness to welcome them." Some admittedly exploited such customs and were parasites, but then, asks the Swami, "what other establishments cost less or achieve more for the sanctification of life?" The Swami also speaks of the imperceptible manner in which our wandering holy men have helped to knit the country together despite its many languages and regional cultures. Such an apologia was required for the English reader when the memoir was first published; it is equally relevant for the reader in India as we prepare to enter the next millennium.

But first and foremost, *An Indian Monk* is the story of one man's spiritual quest and of his trials and tribulations. It is, in fact, the first autobiography (in the modern sense of the word) that we have of a yogi.[1] It moves rapidly, is unsentimental and inspiring, and is

---

[1]Had *An Indian Monk* been published in India as well and been better known, Par-

eminently readable. Its author was a man of indomitable will, capable of great fortitude and austerity. His making as a monk and his description of his experiences and adventures add up to a powerful testament of the truth of yoga. Whoever reads the account of the journey up the 7,000 granite steps of Mt. Girnar, or the visit to the solitary temple at Mahur, or the Swami's adventures and misadventures in the Himalayas, will not think of the sanyasin's life as that of an escapist. The reality of the spiritual path and its complexities and compulsions come across with a vividness and directness all the more startling on account of the brevity of the narrative.

An Indian Monk may be read at many levels and cuts across divisions of taste and interest. It may be studied as an account of a form of society which is fast disappearing. It may be viewed as a book of the supernatural, full of stories of miracles. For many it will be a narrative of adventure which grips and holds the attention from episode to episode. But for the spiritual seeker it is a veritable treasure-house of inspiration and wisdom. It faithfully maps the many changes which mark the life of an aspirant. It touches on the role of diet in one's inner progress and the relevance of celibacy to the spiritual life. What is ardently sought after at one stage, such as sacred books and the company of holy men, may leave one quite indifferent at a later. The memoir, while it dwells on the difficulties of the path, also speaks of its joys and compensations. Chapter 17 describes the higher sensations and pleasures of the inner life, besides which those of the outer pale into insignificance: "The more I concentrated my attention on the Lord, the more beautiful were the forms I beheld floating in the light, so much so that those who pass for beautiful upon this earth appeared ugly." The other senses found similar fulfilment. "Food or no food", the author "relished

---

amhansa Yogananda's publishers would hardly have claimed that *Autobiography of a Yogi* marked "the first time that a great Hindu yogi has written a detailed account of his life." It is interesting that both Purohit Swami and Yogananda were led to write their memoirs in order to bring the truths of yoga alive to western seekers. The two works often cover similar ground but differ greatly in their style. *An Indian Monk* is far less discursive and its narrative moves swiftly; in fact, it is almost a third the length of *Autobiography of a Yogi*.

savours which ravished the sense" and "enjoyed the sweet odours of several flowers when none were present." The body "thrilled with a sense of contacts" and the inner ear was glued to an orchestral music which "no one was playing" and though it performed "hour after hour, there was nothing to pay." We also have a graphic account of the first awakening of the kundalini, a sort of trial by fire: "The flesh was an agony; the senses coals of fire; with bones shattered to pieces, blood boiling; ... my whole frame received electric shocks difficult to sustain."

An Indian Monk also deals with the subject of yogic powers at some length. Even as a child, Purohit had clear evidence of the special powers which some holy men commanded and would have "been the greatest fool on earth had [he] not believed in them." But the more he matured, the more he developed a "strong revulsion" against their use for worldly ends. He delighted in Ramdas Swami's comment on the yogi who walked across the waters of the Krishna, "This is a wonderful feat indeed worth exactly one halfpenny, for which sum the ferryman would have taken the sadhu across." The Swami speaks of the power of physical healing which he developed through his spiritual progress. The desire to alleviate suffering makes the temptation to use such power quite compelling. But Purohit came to realise that "To use spiritual power for finite ends would only distract me from pursuing relations with the infinite." If exploited it would "give out,' leaving one' a spiritual bankrupt."

Next to the difficulties and temptations which beset the spiritual path, the subject which comes for most extended treatment in Purohit Swami's memoir is the unique and complex relationship which knits the aspirant to the adept. At its heart is the mystery whereby the human is divinised. This relationship transcends and absorbs into itself all other relationships. For the disciple the guru is at once his Best Friend, his Beloved, his Lord and Master. His will must become the disciple's will, his every wish a divine command which must be fulfilled. For Purohit Swami, the guru was "my living God, my divine Self, my incarnate Brahma"; or as Bahina Bai sang of her Beloved Sant Tukaram:

He who sets Tukoba's bodily organs in motion is truly Pan-

durang. Tukoba's eyes are also Pandurang. His ears are Pandurang in the form of the *Abhang*.
Whatever Tukoba's hand writes, that is clearly Pandurang. All the actions of Tukoba are Hari, who makes him one with Himself, through the fact of non-duality.[1]

He who has found such a Friend is never alone even in the heart of the remotest jungle. A single love glance from such a Beloved can dissolve barriers on the inner path which have vexed one for months and years, perhaps for many a lifetime.

In making his Master's will his own and becoming one with him, the disciple at last becomes one with the Creator. When this transformation of the human into the divine has been accomplished, even a chance wish of the aspirant becomes God's will, the law and order of the Universe. Purohit Swami, as his palm-leaf horoscope had predicted, lived to attain this apotheosis, and his pilgrimage to Gokul provides the climactic moment of his memoir. Finding the Jamuna placid and the scene quite tranquil, he suddenly yearned that he might behold the scene as it had greeted Krishna's nativity: "I must see! I will not move unless I see." Before he could revoke this impetuous prayer, it was "already answered":

The heavens were pitch dark, the thunder rolled around, and within fifteen minutes of my reaching that spot, torrents of rain fell; the Jamuna grew boisterous, the lightning flashed, the wind roared, the peacocks danced with joy, and in amazement people ran pell mell for shelter. Left alone on the bank, my arms folded, I repeated the Upanishads, and watched the ferocious Jamuna and her terrifying waves.

The text of *An Indian Monk* has been reset for this edition. The original notes and the somewhat idiosyncratic spelling of certain place-names have been retained. But diacritical marks for Indian words and names have been dropped and some typographical

---

[1] *Bahina Bai: Autobiography and Verses*, trans. Justin E. Abbott (Poona: Scottish Mission Industries, 1929), pp. 20-1.

errors have been corrected. A few notes have been added where they seemed desirable as also an index. The frontispiece excepted, the illustrations are original to this edition.

Vinod Sena

Delhi
10 March, 1992

1

How the Soil had been Prepared

I WAS born at Badnera, near Amraoti, in Berar, in the Central Provinces, on the 12th October 1882, of a religious and wealthy family. My grandfather[1] had been a millionaire; he used to ride an elephant, and had fifty palanquins in his house. He held the Customs contract for the Nizam's dominions and was greatly honoured everywhere. His headquarters were at Bhir. After his death, my uncle, the elder stepbrother, wanted to take the whole property, to the detriment of my father, Dadasahib. My father, who was then a boy of eight, said: "Our father amassed this wealth; he is no more. I loved him, not his riches!" and he left the house with his mother and went to his maternal uncle's house at Dhavadshi in the Satara district. So firm was his faith in his Karma that without regret he renounced his claim to a large fortune. I am his son. Little wonder, therefore, if I renounced everything for the sake of God. I had only a short step to take.

On her side, my mother also was balked of her share in the property of her father by her relatives. She never contested for her rights, but resigned herself patiently to the working of the will of God. She had absolute faith in Him, and used to say that if anything belonged to her it must of necessity come to her, for no power on earth could rob her of anything really her own. I sucked the milk of this divine recklessness from her breast.

My father's mother, to whom in my childhood I owed so much, was a highly spiritual soul. She bore this great straitening of her mode of life with resignation, for her son's sake. She found consolation in meditating on Shri Mahalakshmi, the Goddess of Prosperity. She had brought her jewellery with her to her brother's house,

---

[1]Sadashiv Purohit. His elder son was named Krishnarao.

and as she was his senior was looked on as the head of the household. As soon as my father was fifteen, he refused to touch his mother's money, saying: "A woman's property is sacred in India." Therefore he took service on the railway at 15 rupees, or £1 : 2s., per month, on which his maternal uncle had also found employment at a higher salary. For a lad bred in luxury to work as an ordinary servant for such low pay is indeed a trial, but he underwent it rather than continue to be a burden on his mother.

In unspoilt rural India every relative is of divine value to the family, each member of which is expected to make an adequate sacrifice for the whole. They labour together to create the common happiness, and this means the self-abnegation of each, since there is no love without reciprocal sacrifice. The head of a family receives that position in trust from God, and looks to Him for guidance and approval in discharging his duties. The son adores the mother as the visible Goddess, and his father as incarnate God, and his preceptor as a manifestation of divine wisdom. Thus an atmosphere of reverence, purity and sacrifice is generated. Our servants too were members of the living whole. Whenever there was a marriage among them, we paid for it: when death visited them it was our privilege to console. Their lives were intimately interwoven with ours. Service was not a bargain though it was paid, and so saturated with love that both parties enjoyed it, for both believed in Seva-Dharma, the religion of service.

Even the animals were honoured and had their days of worship. Nay, the trees are sacred to the Hindus; the plough, the seeds, the weapons, the sun, the moon and the birds are all divine. The children receive the names of the various gods, and are welcomed as a reincarnation of the Divine Spirit. Mothers sing the songs of Lord Shrikrishna when they are rocking their children's cradles, and each thinks that her baby is none other than a little Holy Krishna, the greatest incarnation in history. In fact, all the phases of life are spiritualised. All desires and passions are means to one end, the spiritual realisation of the divine in each individual. The wife adores her husband as her Lord, and the husband adores her as Lakshmi—the Goddess—the Divine Queen, for with the Hindus marriage is not a contract but a sacrament. It is the union, not of bodies, but of souls that are trying to rise into the divine consciousness. The wife thinks that the husband reincarnates in her son, and hence both parents strive to lead a pure life in order to free the soul of their son for a still greater purity. They think that a spiritual soul born into a family not only emancipates itself but helps to free the souls of the parents and of the whole family and shorten the suffering lives of their Karma. Therefore the mother is very particular in observing certain vows, and makes them rules of conduct that tend to increase the spiritual atmosphere about her. She is anxious that the pre-natal influences should be holy. She reads the sacred books, listens to the sacred stories of the Mahatmas, visits temples, gives alms to the deserving and creates thus a halo of spiritual light about the child before it is born. For both husband and wife have promised each other that they will always be one in devotion, in desire, in monetary circumstances and in their final spiritual emancipation. The devout Hindu is always seeking divine at-one-ness in all the various aspects of life, which is the outward manifestation of the holy spirit, or else its travesty and disguise.

Before I was born, my grandmother, her sister, her brother, his wife, his sons, my father and my mother, all lived in a roomy house at Badnera, the compound of which spread out behind those of our neighbours on the village street. Our house had two storeys, and was built of brick and roofed steeply with rolling tiles that the heavy rains might be immediately carried away. Behind it was a one-storey building for the servants, though several of ours lived in houses of their own scattered about the large village. Still farther back stood the great cattle-shed. There were no fences, but a wide verandah in front of our living-rooms, with steps up to it from the forecourt, for guests and the master. The entrance for the servants was behind the house, and was reached by a lane on the right at the end of which stood the well. We had ample flower and produce gardens besides grazing meadows and fields of wheat. Life there was so generous that my grandmother's worship of the Goddess of Prosperity seemed the most fitting symbol of it, and yet she herself must have compared our conditions with those of her husband's mansions, and found them meagre enough.

2

Grandmother and Nursing Mothers

MY grandmother, Akkasahib, stood so high in the favour of her goddess that when her brother was seriously ill and the physicians had given him up, she prayed and argued with her goddess until the hoped-for answer came. She and Shri Mahalakshmi were at one. She had visions of her, consulted her face to face, and was consoled by her. In very deed her whole life was spiritualised. Though a woman moving through this world, she was in it, not of it.

People who were in doubt how to act came to Akkasahib. She consulted her goddess, and the reply always proved correct. She was extremely beautiful, moved like a queen through the house, and was so benevolent that the whole village held her in reverence. When her husband was taken away, almost every worldly desire had departed from her, and she looked forward to the other world. She led a consecrated life, ate only once a day and then but little, and like a typical Hindu widow, was always cheerful and happy.

Piece by piece she sold her jewellery of considerable worth and spent the money in doing good, especially looking after the comforts of the Swamis and Mahatmas who wandered our country. If any man was without food, he could go to her; there was always enough for him. In fact, my father used to visit the temple in the village every morning and enquire if there was anyone there who wanted food. Such is the religious duty of every householder in India, and my grandmother observed it very carefully. In consequence, so many good people came that in our home the spiritual atmosphere was well nourished.

When two daughters had been born before me, Akkasahib grew restless. She yearned for a grandson. The Brahmins were asked to pray to Lord Shiva to bless the family with a son. The sacred Vedas were chanted, Brahmins were fed with lavish dinners, and everything that could be done, was done. My mother observed her rules of penance strictly. Every day my father worshipped Lord Shiva with a view to obtaining a religiously minded son. The absence of an heir cast a shadow over the family joy. Various gods, in the many temples, had been petitioned, and one day at noon, when the sun was blazing in the sky, I was born.

Sweetmeats were distributed throughout the village in honour of my birth, as is the custom. My mother thought herself the happiest woman on earth, and my grandmother gave presents to the servants that they might share in her joy. My father rushed to the astrologer, and when the latter drew the horoscope and told him that his son was a highly spiritual soul, and that he would one day carry the message of Truth throughout the length and breadth of the world, he was more than happy.

I have since been told how, when according to kindly custom, mothers came to visit my mother, and the babies were passed round that they might benefit by other milks, a Mahratta lady, Janki Bai, belonging to the warrior class, wished to suckle me, but my grandmother said: "You eat eggs, and fish and meat, and onions and other forbidden foods;—do you think that we can let you nurse our son?" Now that lady, whose son, born much at the same time with me, was already dead, had taken so great a fancy to me that she conformed exactly to all our prescriptions, and a few days later had the pleasure of giving me her breast. For selfishness is not even permitted in a mother with respect to her child, and our mothers are true sisters to one another.

Still more beautiful was the devotion shown to me by Bhuti, the cow. She would not allow her calf to suck her, unless I had first done so. As soon as she returned from the jungle every evening, she rushed into the house and would not go to her shed till I had had my meal. She continued to nourish me till I was eight years old, when one day, to my grief, she fell from the ruined fort and died. I shall never forget my cow foster-mother so long as there is breath in me.

I am not to be a Landlord

THE human being whom I knew best on the face of this earth was my grandmother. Passing almost all my time with her, I was obliged to get up early in the morning. In the rainy season the weather was extremely cold, in summer it was overpoweringly hot; but there was no compromise. It was a religious duty to ease oneself first, next to wash the teeth, and then to have a bath and, last, to enter the worship-room. Akkasahib sang the beautiful hymns, and I used to prostrate myself before God and repeat the hymns in my own way, offer the flowers, take the holy water, apply it to my eyes and head, sprinkle it all over my body, and have a share in the food-offerings that were made to Him. Then I had to salute the priest, my grandmother, the elders, my parents and the guests. Nobody was allowed to taste food before all this had been observed, nor was I allowed to run about, and a wonderful charm was cast over the coming day by this ceremonious commencement, which was never cut short or omitted. It made everybody cheerful and happy.

Well, I was fondled by everybody; and though this pleased me, it had a very bad effect on my temper. I could not tolerate that anybody should find fault with me. Once, when my father rebuked me for my folly, I got wild and angry, and buried myself in a silent corner of a room on the upper floor, and left everybody miserable. They ransacked the compound for me. They thought somebody had murdered me for the sake of the jewellery I wore. They searched the well and sent many runners through the village, but I was nowhere to be found. I had had no food since the morning, and it was late when my mother inadvertently went into the very room where I lay and stumbled upon me, and her joy was immense.

I am not to be a Landlord

One day, when somebody was angry with me, I went sullenly to the well and sat on the brink, with my legs hanging loosely inside. They were all in terror lest I should throw myself down. Thus my egoism was fed, and I became a tyrant.

I remember when I was bitten by a cobra my grandmother at once sent for the snake-charmer. He did his best, repeated the sacred words, gave me handfuls of chillies and nimb leaves to eat, and I was cured. He had already cured thousands of such cases, and mine only added one to the many. But Akkasahib had gone to her worship-room, and wrested a reply from her goddess, and came out with the good news and a smile, to learn that the snake-charmer had cured me. If anyone asked me what cured me, the snake-charmer's mantrams or my grandmother's prayers, I would answer: "God cured me. He has cured many by the snake-charmer's spells and others in answer to my grandmother's prayers. How can I say which moved Him?"

After I had been cured I used to visit the snake-charmer's house, and saw a great many serpents playing and frisking in one of his rooms, the door of which always stood open, but they dared not traverse the line he had traced on the floor and come and pay us a visit. We were forbidden to enter the room, but we could enjoy watching them from the door. Whenever a cobra was found in any house, the charmer was sent for. He called aloud, and lo! it came out of its hole, humble and submissive, and the man took it by the hood, and added it to those in his room. Everybody said he was well versed in mantrams—the sacred words or spells.

The Swamis came and came, and were always treated with special respect. I was fond of them, at first because they gave me sweetmeats. I remember one incident as vividly as if it had happened only yesterday. I importuned a Swami to give me sugar-candy. He had none, but I begged all the harder. The Swami silently thrust his hand under the cushions on which he was sitting, and took out a handful of sugar-candy and gave it to me. Boy-like, I wondered how this candy came to be under the cushions. As soon as he went to his bath, I took off the covering, and ransacked the cushions, but there was no trace of any. A little later I was again asking him for candy, and lo and behold! he did just what he had done before. This set my curiosity rolling like a ball; so I used to make sure that there was no candy before the Swami came in, and when he came asked for more candy, and never in vain. Ultimately, quite baffled, I consulted my grandmother. She smiled and scolded me for my indiscretion and said: "You are such a naughty boy! Do not tease the Swami for such petty things. To be a Swami means a great deal more than to provide trifles." This so impressed me that I have never ridiculed any religious man, for I thought: "Who knows, he may be a real Mahatma!"

My grandmother wanted me to be a landlord and gave much of her jewellery to bring waste land under cultivation in the Indore State; but the venture proved a failure. She purchased land near Badnera, enough to keep me above want, but after her departure her brother sold it to furnish his own needs. I was not to be a landlord; I was to be a monk.

Such was the atmosphere in which I was born and bred. There were religious ceremonies and celebrations throughout the year. The Brahmins chanted the Vedas every day. Any man could safely depend upon our house for his food. Mahatmas stayed there. I used to sit at their feet, and do little services for them, though we had a pack of servants. The service of the Mahatmas was a privilege and a pleasure, and silently worked its due result, which was my faith.

Akkasahib told the household one morning that she would leave us at noon. When they told me, I asked: Where would she go? Everybody looked sad. She had asked them to finish their meal, and be ready for her departure. With a heavy heart they obeyed, because obedience was the law of the house. I remember I was wonder-struck to find that people did not eat a full meal as usual. But I had no such idea, and did full justice to mine, and when I went to the room of my grandmother, I found her lying on a woollen carpet, and all the people gathered around her in a solemn mood, and the priest chanting the Vedas from the worship-room.

Akkasahib asked me to come near and said: "My best-beloved child, you have served me very well. May the Goddess bless you! You shall, by her Grace, know the Truth"; and she placed her palm on my head. I did not understand what was to happen.

She asked her brother to tear off her pillow-slip, and lo! there was a fine gold-laced garment in it, and she asked him to spread it on her body, for it belonged to her beloved husband. He did accordingly.

I am not to be a Landlord

She blessed everybody, then asked for the water of the Ganges, drank it, and, with the name of the Goddess on her lips, passed away.

A void was created in my brain. She had been my all in all. They removed me to another room, and to my incessant queries only replied: "She has gone to the House of God." I was only eight years old and could not understand the full significance of that scene then nor for long after. Yet the shock I underwent wrought a very marked improvement in my temper; she had given me her blessing, the very thing I most needed and should now most desire had I not received it.

4

You are a Brahmin; be a Brahmin Always!

SO LONG as Akkasahib had been alive, the house was full. Everybody was happy. There was a smile everywhere. But as soon as she was gone, the household split up. My father was transferred to Zhansi;[1] my grandmother's brother, Bhaoosahib, to Bina. Akkasahib's sister Maisahib went to Benares for good; she was only living with us for her sister's sake. The servants, weeping bitterly, were discharged, and as the stars had decreed, the house which had been so full was soon empty. The cows were given to the Brahmins, the buffaloes and bullocks were sold, the fields were leased out, certain things were distributed among neighbours, the house was left in charge of a friend. The mothers who had suckled me sobbed; the whole village, which had been fed with our love, felt sad; and my parents took me to Zhansi, up in the North, immortal in history as the place where the greatest woman warrior, Queen Laxmibai, fought for the independence of India. The Great Indian Peninsular Railway had lent my father as organising expert to the Indian Midland Railway.

My father was now the head of an office, and naturally was very busy organising his new staff. Dadasahib talked very little, and only on grave subjects, though he was always kind and courteous, benevolent and hospitable. He never told a lie, never owed any man even a farthing, never disturbed the peace of anyone and never allowed anybody to disturb his, and he never looked at the face of a woman except my mother. He always walked in the streets with downcast eyes. He had seen the feet of the wives of his best friends,

---

[1] Jhansi. In many parts of India the Z sound is often replaced by the one for J. The Zanskar Range is often called Jhanskar in Ladakh. *Editor.*

but not their faces. He had to suffer on account of his virtue, but used to say: "Virtue is its own reward. Those who expect a reward for theirs injure its purity and insult its nature. Virtue gives you self-satisfaction, and the riches you go without are compensated in contentment". He performed his religious duties regularly, went to the temple every day, and led the life of a householder according to the Hindu scriptures.

My mother, into whose arms I was thrown by the death of my grandmother, was now all in all to me. The pleasure of having a son had been practically denied her so long as the grandmother was there. She was by nature amiable and kind; she fed me, clothed me, prayed for me, and allowed me to sleep in her blessed arms. I worshipped her as my deity and sucked the milk of devotion through her presence. At times I wept because she was out of my sight.

I remember how one custom exerted a powerful influence over my mind. Whenever I came back from school, from play or from some ceremony, I wanted to dash in, but was always stopped, for they would not allow me to enter the house before somebody had come out with a piece of bread, passed it round my face in the air, and thrown it into the street, in order to remove any evil influences. Also whenever I felt out of sorts, my mother came with salt, chillies and mustard seed in her hands, and passed these through the air, all round my body; she then threw the whole handful on to the fire, and to my astonishment it generally emitted a dirty smell. It irked me to sit quiet while this ceremony was in progress, but my mother used to persuade me, saying: "My child, you always feel better after I have done it. It is for your good. You do not know how many evil forces are working in this world. Consciously or unconsciously, they act on you, and you can see that if I put a small piece of a chilli on the fire, it makes so strong a stench that it is impossible for you to remain in the house. But now you see that many chillies are burning quietly in the fire, and emitting only a slight dirty smell." I tried it, tested it, and found that there was something which I could not understand. But in India, thousands of mothers still perform this ceremony in order to ward off evil influences from their child, and I saw that children who were fretful and crying miserably began to smile once the ceremony had been performed.

Dadasahib was too serious for me, and I was afraid to approach him. I always stood in his presence with downcast eyes, and listened to his words of wisdom. Such was the honour which I paid my father. When I was with my mother, I used to roll on her lap, tease her and harass her for little things, and with a vengeance loved her. Dadasahib moved on a higher plane; my mother moved on this earth, and that is the reason why I was so fond of her.

I enjoyed listening to the addresses given by our family priest in a neighbouring temple. He always invoked the authority of the great epics, *Mahabharata*, the *Devi-Bhagwata*, the *Ramayana*, the *Geeta*, and I, though understanding little else, was deeply interested in all the narratives. Especially that episode where the Pandavas are exiled to the forests moved me more than I can tell, and that other when Droupadi was harassed in open court, and ultimately Lord Shrikrishna came to the rescue.

In April the festival of Shri Ramachandra lasted for ten days. The most important events of his life were rendered with word, action, dance, music and song, so that an indelibly vivid impression lives on in my mind. At Amraoti where thousands gathered to see, a platform was erected on which, under the shade of a vast awning, the players performed, and the notables leaned against piles of cushions to watch them. This island of shadow was surrounded by the multitude squatting on the ground. The magnificent costumes and costly jewellery were lent by the wealthy. Only boys and men performed; villagers and men from the small towns coveted the honour of being allotted even a small part. The great Hero was supposed to have delivered even his enemies from further Karma, so even those who took bad characters felt that they shared in the triumph for holiness enacted.

When Shri Ramachandra has defeated all save the last of the chieftains leagued against him, Mandodari, the wife of this last Ravana, says to her husband: "He is an incarnation of the Lord—why do you not surrender?" but he replies: "What? surrender my redemption! When he kills me, I who complete his triumph shall share in it. I will fight with all my might that His glory may be the greater".

At Badnera the crowd was comparatively small and the performances could take place in a temple court. The life of Lord Shrikrishna was given in August under a temple roof, as then the

You are a Brahmin; be a Brahmin Always!

rains pour down. I still clearly see a small boy with beautiful features dressed as the Lord playing on his flute while the cowherds, his young disciples, listened in ravishment to those enchanting tunes.

The anniversary of Lord Dattatreya fell in December, the finest month of the year; not only the preacher, but all the least spectators, like myself, saw the holy child, and felt as though the Divine Mother permitted their eyes to kiss the lotus feet. Worship and pleasure were the same thing and equally free; the expenses were defrayed by voluntary contributions, and if any deficit remained the head men in the village or the wealthy in the towns made it good. There were also Samkeertans performed by a single actor-dancer, accompanied by a few musicians and singers. During the first hour he preached the doctrine; during the second he acted, sang and danced anecdotes illustrative of it. Thus art and religion were at one, and each too humble to scorn the other.

Thus the foundations of my faith were laid on the admiration of my eyes, ears and heart; and soul danced with body with an ease and naturalness like that of the changing seasons. O what a happy childhood was mine!

My *munj*, or the Brahmin sacred-thread ceremony, was performed at Zhansi when I was nearly nine. So many guests had assembled that other houses had to be taken to accommodate them, as we then lived in a far smaller house that at Badnera. There was feasting and rejoicing. The Vedas were chanted, and the Brahmins were paid generously. I remember the day when my father preached to me the sacred Gayatri mantra, and said in a serious tone: "My child, henceforth you are a Brahmin; be a Brahmin always!" He gave me his blessings, and the Brahmins followed suit. I really thought that I was a Brahmin, a superior, sacred being. I was taught the Vedas—a great joy for me! I loved to repeat them. I do not know the reason, but every time I repeated my prayers I thought I became purer than before. Even today, whenever I listen to the Vedas or the Upanishads, I lose myself in joy; I think that I am transported to another sphere, and partake of spiritual sustenance. Salutations to the Vedas, the earliest of all inspired words!

My father worked honestly and strenuously, so much so that he fell seriously ill. He got an attack of asthma, and was treated by many a physician, but to no effect. Ultimately he left Zhansi for Poona, and submitted himself to the treatment of an Indian doctor, and was cured. Hundreds of rupees had been spent to obtain the services of English doctors, but he was cured by a man of eighty, with a medicine worth a few pennies. Then he lost all faith in British pharmacopoeia, and turned towards Indian medicine in times of emergency.

He refused to return to Zhansi from Poona because he said the climate did not suit him. He was offered a rise from 300 rupees to 500 a month, but refused, and to the surprise of all accepted a clerkship at 20 rupees, or £1:8s., per month at Amraoti. He made this sacrifice for my sake, as he wished me not to forget my native Marathi. He was head of an office at Zhansi; he became an ordinary clerk again at Amraoti. Laying stress on the principle of Karma, he said: "Everybody tries to find happiness through money. I do not believe in it. Real happiness lies within you." So we came back to within five miles from the old village and we rented five rooms in a much larger house.

5

Mahatmas and the Divine Master in a Cobra

SOON I was a pupil at an Anglo-Vernacular school. Rising very early in the morning, after my bath and worship, I had my breakfast with many sweets, then went out to play before my father got up; came back only to find him in his worship-room, took my lunch with me, and went to school. After my return, I had dinner, and went to bed before my father came home from the Club. I was afraid of him. He was a stoic, a strict disciplinarian, and my reserve with him was as great as my freedom with my mother.

He enquired about me, and my mother gave the necessary replies. One evening he came very early, and summoned me before him, and asked me to read my English lessons. I was shaking with fear. I read nearly eighteen lessons of the First Primer of English, one after another; he asked me to translate, and I rattled it off. My father suspected that something was wrong, since I did not turn pages correctly. He took the book in his hand, pointed out a lesson, and asked me to read. I could not. I was silent. He understood I was repeating all the lessons by heart, without even knowing the two alphabets. He laughed and laughed till my mother ran into the room to know why. Pointing to me he said to her: "Look at your best-beloved son! He knows all the lessons by heart, but we must engage a teacher to teach him the alphabet." I perspired profusely. That very same night my father gave me my first lesson in English, and I began to read and write.

I was eleven and only too much of a boy. Having every possible luxury at home, I received no pocket-money when I went to school. Other boys bought sweets with theirs, and distributed them in the interval. I envied them, and once, seeing an eight-anna piece laid before the household goddess, took it, bought sweets and distributed them, and was as popular as any boy. But the silver coin was missed. My father asked if I had taken it. I said "No", but the truth was discovered. He ordered me to strip off my fine clothes, and I had to wear a poor boy's coat for a whole year, nor would my father look at me or speak to me all that time. On that first night I had to stand on the terrace shivering till three in the morning, when through the intervention of my mother I was taken inside the house. It was a terrible lesson, and produced such an effect on me that I never dared tell a lie again. I learnt the art of discipline at the feet of my august father.

While at the English school I used to meet a Mahatma, who looked as if he were fifteen and was always stark naked. Some took him for a lunatic, others thought him a saint. He was the only son of a rich Marwari banker. His parents were very religious, and worshipped the Lord Shiva. They had been childless. They tried all things, all with no result. One day a sanyasin came to their door and begged for food. He was royally entertained. On the eve of his departure he asked his hosts what he could do for them. They with suppliant attitude said: "We have got everything in this world, health, wealth and honour, but we have no son to look after our spiritual welfare when we leave this body. We desire to be blessed with one." The Mahatma replied: "What sort of a son do you want? A worldly boy with a long life, or a highly spiritual soul with a short one?" They were religious and said they would like to have a saint. The Mahatma went away after having given them a blessing, and here was the result: a son who had no attachment to anything whatsoever. He lived anywhere and everywhere, begged for his food, laughed when he was ridiculed, was silent when he was extolled, had neither garment nor home, but everywhere found homes for himself. Some well-known materialists well nigh worshipped him. They felt very happy when they sat near his feet. He talked always about Brahma. At times he talked like a learned man, and discussed with academical perfection. One man in particular, a friend of my father, told me he was always attracted by the perfume that emanated from his breath. Boys are after all boys, and there were some who ridiculed him, but I always paid him honour, and attributed to his agency many dreams in which I saw him

Mahatmas and the Divine Master in a Cobra

smiling and at peace; these came to me a few days after he left his body, and I was elevated and harmonised.

My father and I were visiting Bhaoosahib at Bina. Thither came a Mahatma one morning, and was very cordially received. He was naked, but after a few minutes people flocked to the house, bringing very costly dresses. He wore them all, one after another for a few minutes each, then gave them back to be treasured by their owners as heirlooms. People came and came, and listened to him day after day. At times he fell silent, at others he talked and talked. But he always said what was exactly appropriate to the several needs of his hearers. Though every man came full of his trouble, none ever dared to breathe a word about it. Yet the reply came, and they each got satisfaction. It would have been superfluous to ask any question; the Mahatma knew. His voice was musical, and it still rings in my ears. I was always with him. Frequently I could not understand his changes of mood, but dared not question him.

One day this Mahatma drew me to him and said: "Well, my beloved child, what do you want me to do for you?" On the spur of the moment I answered: "I would like to have a pearl necklace to wear." He laughed and said: "My boy, you see that I am a naked man, and have not a garment of my own to wear. These people have lent me theirs." I retorted: "Then ask somebody to lend you a pearl necklace." He grew serious, then asked us all to shut our eyes, and after a minute when we opened them we saw a beautiful necklace on a silver tray, with a silken shawl under it. The Mahatma took the necklace in his hand, place it round my neck, and asked me whether I was satisfied. I said: "Yes, but now tell me where it came from. I do so want to know." He gave me the address of a Bombay pearl merchant and asked me to write and tell him where his necklace was and not to worry about it, for it would be brought back to him by the next train. The reply telegram came, and this set my mind completely at rest. My father sent the necklace back to Bombay by one of his friends. He took care the next day to rebuke me for over-familiarity with the Mahatma.

I sat up with this Mahatma. The doors were locked, as there was danger from the dacoits in Bina then, and at midnight we went to bed. In the morning we found he was gone; yet the locks were intact, though my father, anxious to spare his uncle by rendering whatever service he could, had locked up and put the keys under his pillow. How the Mahatma went was a great mystery for all of us. To have had his blessing before going to bed gave me great contentment. A wire was sent to Saugor, and the reply came that he was in the jungle as usual.

My father was in the habit of reading the *Guru-Charitra*, or the Life of the Divine Master. At one period, every day after he had left the worship-room a big cobra entered the house and occupied the very seat in which he had been sitting. I had once been bitten by a cobra, and that had struck terror in me. But my father, with a calmness peculiarly his own, took me outside the house and said: "The Divine Master Himself has come in the form of a cobra. This house belongs to Him as much as to us. We will enter it again when it pleases Him to go." Nobody was allowed to kill the cobra, and when he silently crept out of the house we silently crept into our beds. It happened nearly a dozen times, and in the end took away the last vestige of my fear of snakes. I was a great coward when a child, and this is how the cowardice slowly began to leave me.

It was the rule of the house to go to the temple every day and pray. I went regularly, and when the days for the school examination drew near prayed fervently for my success. At other times I prayed God to give me an opportunity of seeing Him. Though I prayed and prayed, and wept, He did not appear. Yearning for the vision made me restless, till there was anguish in my heart, yet I always thought to see Him one day. So many said they had seen Him, then why not I?

6

The Philosophy of Riches

I HAD very few playfellows. My bosom friend was my mother, and my father my most revered teacher. He never talked about himself or our family, nor about official matters, for he used to say: "What is the use of parading our pedigree before people? Why boast that my father rode an elephant, when I have not even an ass to ride on? Nobody belongs to anybody else. Everybody for himself is the grim law of this universe. My father came alone, and he went alone. He enjoyed the fruit of his Karma, and I too shall have to fulfil mine." And if anybody asked him any question as regards official matters, he would answer: "Enough of that! I have worked as an honest slave till evening; I no longer owe service to anybody, and want to enjoy independence till tomorrow morning. Let me breathe some fresh air, and try to possess my soul." He pondered his religion and read many books on it till late into the night, and in his own way was very happy.

He was so very reserved that I remember his saying to me: "It is no use making a host of friends. That is all pure selfishness masquerading in the garb of kindness. They flatter you so long as it serves their personal ends. As soon as you tell them an unpalatable truth, they turn round and begin to hate you. Why run risks in this world? Life is short, and we must make the best of the situation in which we are placed. You must learn at every step and grow wiser everyday. Some people are very fond of enduring the same trials over and over again. They learn nothing and will never be happy till doomsday, since they expect happiness from a quarter where none exists. This world is very poor in friendship, love and sacrifice. Why not worship God instead? He is the fountain-head of all that is holy and good, and by our worship we automatically gain what is pure and beneficial to our eternal welfare."

He used to quote the passage in the *Geeta* where Lord Shrikrishna says: "Thou art thy enemy as well as thy friend." He wanted to make a friend of his soul rather than of anybody else. He was self-poised, and was always willing to give away his possessions in order to make others happy. He knew his own limitations, knew how to control himself and discharge his duties. Even the European officials always held him to be a man of upright character.

And my mother was love incarnate. How ill I deserved her love; always a worry, teasing her for everything. I wanted a novel dish for every meal; I was fond of costly sweets, and she spent much of her time thinking how to indulge me. And when I refused to eat, "To avoid", as I said, "tasting the dish of a week ago", she said mildly: "My beloved child, at times I think you were born in the wrong home. But even if you had been a prince I am sure they could not have given you a surprise dish every hour. Our world is very poor in that respect. In spite of the various combinations that we devise we cannot achieve perpetual variety. The kinds of fruits are limited, and I do not know how to create new ones. In spite of my desire to serve you, I really am helpless. God alone is able to satisfy your desires; nobody else can."

From ten to sixteen I suffered from a colic pain in my stomach, and, having been brought up as a very spoiled child, would fret and pine over petty things. I wanted novelties and failed to digest what was given me. I think I was unhappy because every sort of happiness was mine. I found pleasure in being miserable without a cause. Nevertheless I worshipped God every day, and read the lives of the great Mahratta saints, especially that of Shri Ramdas Swami, the spiritual guide of Shivaji the Great, the founder of the Mahratta Empire, and Shri Eknath Swami, the disciple of Shri Janardan Swami, who was the disciple of Lord Dattatreya. My father worshipped Lord Dattatreya, and received visions of him and asked me to read the *Guru-Charitra* constantly. I think this laid the foundation of my spiritual relations with the Lord. I worshipped Lord Hanuman, the God of Strength, for giving me a little of his power. I petitioned the goddess Mahalakshmi to give me sufficient wealth. From Lord Shiva I besought the power of renunciation, and from Lord Dattatreya the initiation into the science of Atma-Vidya, or Self-knowledge, and prayed all these gods to give me success in my

The Philosophy of Riches

examinations and my life in general.

It may sound ridiculous, but at times I prayed God to do my lessons for me, to answer the problems set me in arithmetic, when at night I felt too tired to solve them, and to my surprise found that He did not condescend to do it. I wondered over this, for He was reported to have helped so may devotees, and I could not understand why He failed in his duty to me, since I thought my devotion very great. Tardily, I came to understand that devotion is quite another thing and that I was really expecting Him to be my slave in return for a little prayer. Or course when my father learnt that I was disappointed because the Lord did not solve the problems of geometry for me, he insisted on a better understanding. Then at last the idea dawned on me that devotion ought to be pure and simple, and that love ought to be unselfish, and that prayer was no bargain. A new light broke in upon my poor distracted nerves, and I began to repent and tried to love Him in the fullness of my heart.

I used to attend the singing parties in temples, and revelled in the various songs of the poet-saints. Every poet was inspired by his self-realisation, and their poetry went home to me. I used to sing their songs constantly, and they brought me great spiritual consolation. In 1897, the year of the great famine, when I was fifteen there were many people in the house, relatives and friends, who were partaking of our hospitality. My father was selling my mother's jewellery at her urgent request and feeding them all. It was his strict order that every man who came to his door should receive a piece of bread. My mother was always busy in the kitchen, and was all commiseration for the starving poor. One day my father came home very discomposed and refused to touch his food. I was wonder-struck; nobody understood why. With stealthy steps, with the permission of my elders, I went to his room to beg him to have his dinner, but saw tears trickling down from his eyes. He controlled himself when he saw me. I told him that the dinner was ready, and with a heavy heart he followed me. He could only eat a few morsels, and retired very early to his bed.

The next day I learnt that he had seen some people dying of starvation, and could not bear the sight. That was why he had wept. I asked my aunt why the rich people in the town allowed them to die? It was a very simple question, but she reported it to my father.

When we assembled the next day for dinner, my father with a smile said: "My child, you wonder why the rich do not feed them. The rich are rich because they do not give. As soon as they begin to give they will become poor. The one qualification for wealth is hoarding."

7

The Great Yogic Powers

I WAS a lean lad, with a bright face, and sparkling eyes that everybody admired. Yet the colic pain in my stomach was unbearable. Six years running I fell ill as the examination approached and was promoted to a higher class on the recommendation of my teachers. I was intelligent but unwilling to study, being interested in everything save my books. Though extremely fond of play, I was ever ready with a sermon on religion. One of my teachers told me before the class: "My dear boy, this is no place for you; go to some temple and preach there. That is what you were born for." The saints and the poets of Maharashtra had taken such a strong hold on my mind that I had no time to study. I fancied it possible to realise the divine life, before doing anything else. But it was not so easy, as I found out later.

One day in the early hours of morning, my father sent for me, took me by the hand, and wanted me to sit on the same cushion with him. I was thunderstruck: never had I sat in his presence, but always stood as a mark of profound reverence. But he told me in a mild tone: "My good friend, today you attain the sixteenth year of your life. According to the scriptures, I must no longer treat you as a son but my friend. Hitherto you have obeyed me, henceforward we are equals and friends. You can discuss every subject with me, and need only act on my suggestions when you feel convinced." Of course I could not sit with him, and have never taken that liberty, but have felt proud of giving him honour by standing, no matter what my learning and age.

I passed the matriculation of the University of Bombay in 1898. The plague was raging furiously at Poona where we had many relatives, so my father sent me to Nagpur to the Morris College in June 1899, and I entered for the Arts course.

Before leaving Amraoti, I visited the various temples to worship, and took ample time to ponder my religion. I was so fond of the goddess Jagadamba that nights passed in weeping because I received no vision of her. Time flew, and still she sent no message. My tears continued copiously, and one night, before I left for Nagpur, she appeared to me in a dream and asked me what I wanted. I was dumbfounded. I only gazed at her. She was such a glorious sight! She waited for an answer, and at last placed her hand on my head, then disappeared. I woke up and found myself quite happy. Henceforth I felt that she was there with her benignity to watch over my interests and ensure my spiritual welfare.

I was free at Nagpur to do whatever I liked. My mother was with me to look after my comforts. My father sent sufficient money: the weight of his presence was lifted from my life, and I found freedom most enjoyable. Physical exercises made me stronger day by day; the colic pain disappeared; my appetite improved. Many friends and a round of social activities gave scope to my individuality and filled me with happiness. The professors loved me, my nature was jovial; everybody liked me, with the very few exceptions of those who felt jealous of my advantages. I wrote poems in Marathi and Sanskrit, spoke in debating societies, played in matches, argued in private and contended for the causes I had espoused at public meetings. On the quiet I helped those who were in need, taught those too poor to pay a tutor, and loved those who wanted my love.

Free as a bird, I moved through the atmosphere of my choice, and was always gay and cheerful. Very little time was left for study. Though my father sent money for the purchase of books I bought none, yet was soon hard up because, being ready to give, I found many as ready to receive. My heart never allowed my intellect to do its work. So I passed my first Arts examination in 1901, without spending a penny on books, and joined the B.A. class and took philosophy as my voluntary subject. Fancying myself as a philosopher, I determined to advance thought by working at this subject.

I rose at 3 A.M. and went straight to the gymnasium with my friends, came back at 5, and was ready to receive anybody at 6. Very few people knew how my mornings were spent. My father had taught me to do things rather than talk about them. I learnt to wrestle and to fence under the guidance of experts and was a prime

The Great Yogic Powers

favourite with my wrestling master, but one day accidentally I brought him down, and he felt very humiliated. I with reverence touched his feet and apologised, and seeing that he could not get over it, said I would never use his art again, as I had no wish to triumph over him. At length he saw I was in earnest and was comforted. Never since he was a man had he been thrown, and I have never wrestled with anybody since. Scholars had become associated with feeble physique, cowardice and early death, and a generation of athletes was in fashion as a result of the reaction. As a scholar-athlete I felt bound to be the champion of learning, and was peculiarly sensitive to the gibes of "the bloods." The fault in my armour, which gave them the best chance of touching me home, was my inability to swim, which they attributed to cowardice; so on three several occasions I threw myself into a deep tank, whence I could only be rescued on rising for the third time; then, my mother took a vow from me that I would never do it again. I had shown them, at least, that I knew how to drown myself and had the courage to take the risk.

I had my lunch at 11 A.M. and went to College always an hour late. But the Professor of English, Mr. Ganguli, was so partial to me that he would tell me with a smile that he had marked me present.

I went to the College with only notebook and pencil. One day Suresh Chandra Roy, the Professor of Philosophy, was taking his class. I had had a heavy meal that day and fell asleep, and began to snore. Of course the professor woke me up and asked me to stand. I felt utterly humiliated. He asked me whether I possessed any books of philosophy; I said no. He asked me whether I had read any; I said no. He asked me whether I appeared for any weekly examinations; I said never. He was angry and said I must appear for the coming examination.

I hurried to a friend of mine, asked him to coach me up in the books, read them, and within two days' time I went over the whole course taught in three months and appeared for the examination. The professor was so highly pleased with my answers that not only did he read my paper in the class, but he told me that I need no longer attend, and that he would mark me always present in spite of my absence. It was a great triumph for me. Henceforth we became great friends. We discussed and discussed, and ultimately he told in confidence: "My dear boy, I do not think these books on philosophy will help you in achieving what you wish to attain. They are all dry bones. You must go to some yogi, who can initiate you in the processes of life. These academical discussions cannot help any longer. You are growing now, and growing very rapidly, and these little clothes which suited you for a time, are outgrown. Go to a Mahatma, a living saint. He will lead you towards your goal." And he took me to the Shri Shankaracharya of Shiva-Ganga-Dhama, and I found he was a great yogi, and I discussed and argued with him. He replied very patiently, and I felt satisfied for a time. He was not only well versed in the various schools of philosophy, but was a great yogi who practised meditation. I used to visit him every morning and evening, and was very glad to have met him.

Debating with all the ardour that I could command, persuaded me that I was very intelligent and even—oh, the pity of it!—that I was wise. But disillusionment came. I had no peace of mind. The more I fed my intellect with academic learning, the more I became intoxicated with self-conceit, and was led into darkness instead of light. This made me more and more restless. My brain grew feverish; slowly and surely my physical strength began to assert itself in the wrong way. I put on flesh every day, but that added fuel to my temptations. Throwing aside my books, I pondered over my situation, physical, moral and spiritual, and felt it necessary to correct my habits before it should be too late, since I was losing ground.

In search after yogis, I quite accidentally stumbled on a Mahatma. He lived in an old house with a few disciples, and was not very well known because he cared nothing for name and fame. When I saw him I prostrated myself, and with folded hands begged of him to give me light, as I was immersed in darkness. He seemed to like my humility. We talked, and I was more than satisfied with him, for he spoke words which were the direct outcome of his realisation. He spoke what he knew. He was in direct touch with the Divine Master. In the remotest recesses of my heart I thought it would be a grand thing if he would give me a practical illustration of some of the yogi powers described by the great sage Bhagwan Patanjali in his aphorisms of yoga. When we were about to part, he took me by the hand and asked me to see him the next morning, as he wanted to show me something that would interest me. I did not understand what he meant, yet was sure that he was thinking of fulfilling my desire.

The next morning I was there and was shown into a room. It had only one door, which was of the old strong type, with just a little hole in it of the size of half a crown. His disciples asked me to examine the room. Two of my friends who had come to ridicule tested the ceiling and the walls with a crow-bar and certified their strength. The walls were six feet thick. After a short time the Mahatma, with a gracious smile, came, moving his hand on his long snow-white beard, entered the room alone, placed himself in his yogic posture, and asked his disciples to lock the door from outside. The door was locked, and my friends, who took it as a big hoax, sealed it from outside. We were asked to come again next morning. We did so, and there we saw the Mahatma, with his eyes shut, sitting in the same posture, but hanging without any support in the air. We could see him through the hole in the door. We were all dumbfounded, including some who, having been in England, were materialists. We were asked to come again next morning. As we arrived at the door we met the Mahatma. He looked very bright, and with a smile asked my friends to go to the room and see if their locks and the seals were in order. My friends rushed to the door; everything was intact. They unlocked the padlocks and examined the room very carefully, and found there was no possibility of doubt.

The Mahatma took me into his private room, asked me to sit by his side on the tiger-skin, and said in a loving tone: "My dear child, this is not jugglery. You wanted to test the truth of yoga. You have, and it will be my joy if you try to realise it one day. Everything in this world is false. Brahma alone is real. Then why not give up everything in order to realise Him? Do not ridicule anything. Have faith, and you will succeed." He placed his palm on my head, gave me his blessing in the name of Lord Dattatreya, treated me with sweetmeats, and with light shining in his beautiful eyes, said he wanted to leave in the morning. "Where for?" "Benares. To commit my body to the Ganges!"

We talked till midnight. He went out asking us not to follow. The next morning a wire came from his disciples at Benares saying that

The Autobiography of an Indian Monk

the Mahatma arrived there the previous night, and threw his body peacefully into the sacred Ganges in the morning, when the sun was just peeping over the horizon in the East.

8

The Astrologer's Prediction

SLOWLY and surely I began to lose my faith in books. With all my philosophy I had gained nothing which could be valued in terms of peace. The stronger I became the more passionate I was. The books which deal with sexual love inflamed me. There were many temptations, and I needed constant self-control. Shame burned within me and made my mind weaker every day. I felt drawn towards woman, and could very well understand that I was drifting backwards.

Most of my College friends were married; my mother had returned home to my father. I was lodging with a family and met many ladies, and it was no fault of theirs that I was unusually strong and handsome. One or two among them made advances, but I was a puritan like my father; my response was to forgo all showiness in dress, to grow a beard and gradually to give up food; deciding that most of it was unnecessary, till I lived on one meagre meal a day. Whenever my mind went astray, I used to take a cold bath, then run straight into the worship-room to pray and weep. That gave me temporary relief. I frequented places where religious preceptors preached, where sadhus and fakirs stayed, and passed my time in their company. With the help of two of my friends I conducted a high school and taught there regularly after the College hours were over. I busied myself with public service, trying to do good to my fellows so as never to allow my mind to be idle, for then evil thoughts crept in. I was the son of a father who was a strict moralist, and I held it my first duty to abide by a high standard, both physically and mentally. It was comparatively easy to control the physical, but what about the mind? It wavered and revolted in spite of my strenuous efforts. Unmarried, a strict celibate, I knew that unless my mind were under control all my professions would prove false. My thoughts made me angry; I would scold them, then coax them with spiritual texts into observance of the laws of religion. It was an incessant fight, which used up all my strength.

Whenever I was in the company of religious people my mind calmed, I lost my appetite for new things, there was less charm in life, and I felt disillusioned about my so-called friends. So many proved jealous of me and tried to damage me, as though that would advance themselves. Jealousy had meant nothing to me, nor did I dream that ingratitude often occurred. When my kindness was repaid with unkindness, I was shocked. And the most astounding revelation that I had to face was that people told malicious lies. What on earth for? I saw no reason, I could not conceive any. But the fact remained, and I was forced to probe into the deeper meaning of human nature. Before long I saw it as so much dirty linen, and felt that it more than justified my father in saying: "The less we deal with mankind, the better for our spiritual welfare."

I had thought men virtuous. Now I wanted to ignore their existence altogether; so great a change had been wrought in me. The Mahatmas gave me their support. They went further and said: "This whole world is a myth. Brahma alone is real."

Everybody has limitations. Each weighs the other against himself, and makes no allowance for different situations and capacities. Men are carried away by their sentiments, and that is why they misunderstand. They not only misunderstand, they misinterpret, and thus pervert the evidence. I found the root of the evil difficult to diagnose, but in my mathematics class Professor Bannerjea came to my rescue. Whenever he examined our papers, his sole comment was, "Ignorance." The word became my key; it opened the door for the best solution, dutiful compassion.

Every vacation I used to wander through Maharashtra in search of Mahatmas, and visit the holy places of pilgrimage. I would prostrate myself before anybody and everybody who took up the role of a Mahatma, and tried to sit at his feet and imbibe the spirit of his teachings. I had no power of discrimination, and I thought that no intellectual standard could be applied to their proficiency. Some of them lived in jungles, some in big cities, and led very luxurious lives. Some spoke very little, others too much, and everyone had his peculiar system for imparting knowledge. Some expressed themselves in a few select words, which were unintelligible to all except the blessed soul for whom they were intended. I found it at times very difficult to follow their meaning. This humiliated me. The disciples explained, and I perceived that for all their elucidations I was still in the dark.

I learned how to concentrate all my attention on the few intelligible words that fell from the lips of these holy men. I eagerly waited for them by day and pondered them at night. It gave a new impulse to my spiritual life, and I can certify veraciously that I bore away some truth from every place. Much discussion was current about the spiritual status of these gurus, but I was blind to it. I wanted spiritual light, and I found gleams everywhere, even in those who were not supposed to possess any. For my father always said: "What have you to do with the spiritual status of any man? If you want to enjoy the mango-fruit, it is of no use to discuss the history of the tree. It may be five years old or fifty, it may have been planted by a holy man or a scoundrel, still the fruit is always the same, beautiful and delicious. Eat it and be happy. In this world no man wins praise alone, but gets his share of censure as well. At times people are blamed because they are virtuous. But those who are in search of truth should give no weight to these judgments. They should approach reality directly, and enjoy it face to face." The Mahatmas, I found, never had a word of censure for each other, but there were disciples who thought the best way to praise their Mahatma was to vilify the others.

When I found I could not profit by the teachings of anyone, I quietly withdrew, and attributed my failure to a defect of my own psychology. To pass judgment on everybody is to profess too much. We each have our own intellectual limitations, and we easily ignore these when we diagnose others, or sum them up. I was so keen about my spiritual welfare that I would not allow my mind to taint itself with any evil thoughts. That was practical spirituality, and it made me happy in my own way.

Thus I became acquainted with the various schools of yoga. I read the *Geeta* regularly and began to understand it more and more. I read the *Guru-Charitra*, and it instilled into my heart the great principles of devotion. I read the lives of the saints, and these gave me an incentive to practical life. I practised the yogic postures, and took a few lessons in meditation. I always slept on a grass mat without a pillow, had my two or three baths regularly, went into the temple, repeated the name of God even when in society, trying to keep my mind occupied with the one thought of God. My conscience became very sensitive, and made me aware of my defects. I knew I had to climb the heights of the Himalayas and tried to equip myself with my whole strength in order to qualify myself for the heavy task that lay before me.

I presented myself for the B.A., yet knew I should fail. I had a very bad habit of not answering all the questions in the various papers set by the examiners. As soon as I found that I could secure passable marks, I would give up writing and walk straight out of the hall. I did not want to win either scholarships or prizes, for long ago I had told my father that I did not like to rob poor students of chances of which they had greater need than I. Even my teachers believed what I said.

I did not appear for the geometry paper in matriculation for I was sure that I could secure more than enough marks in arithmetic. I did not solve a single question in algebra, not because I did not know how to do it, but because I knew I could secure sufficient marks in trigonometry; I refused to answer a single question in logic because I was so sure of psychology and moral philosophy. It was a peculiar kind of vanity, and I had to pay for it. I translated into beautiful Sanskrit verse an English passage and wrote it out on the first leaf I sent in without having read in the instructions that nothing on the front page would be examined, and consequently failed of the aggregate number of marks. It was a great defeat, but I had only to thank myself for it.

I took up the position of a teacher at Amraoti, then stood again as private student from Indore and passed successfully, receiving my degree of B.A. from the Calcutta University in 1903.

But when I returned from Indore to Amraoti my father refused to speak to me; he was always sad and serious. The joy of the house was gone, and I could not understand the reason. One day I went to the house of a friend of my father, and we talked about the change in his mood. All of a sudden he burst out and said: "You silly boy! don't you know that you are the cause?" I had no inkling as to what he meant. There was an astrologer sitting by, and he enquired about

The Astrologer's Prediction

me, and was told that I was the son of Dadasahib. He laughed cynically, then said: "You ought to be ashamed of yourself. Look at your father, and look at yourself. He is a most virtuous man, and you, at so early an age, are ....." I now looked at him; he saw that I had the wrong complexion and began to hesitate. Perhaps he had made a miscalculation.

I was upset. I told him in plain language: "With all honour to your knowledge of astrology, let me humbly tell you that I have not touched even a cup of tea, still less of liquor, and you may rest assured that I have never known any woman." My language was more emphatic, and I repented afterwards and apologised for having spoken rudely. But it had the desired effect. He again looked up his almanac, worked out my horoscope, clapped his hands and said: "You are right. I must see your father at once."

We came to our house. I saluted my father, and the astrologer said to him: "My good friend, forgive me. My calculations were wrong. Here is the correct horoscope of your son. I take back whatever I said about him, and have great pleasure in testifying that you are very fortunate in having so spiritual a son, and I can only say that he will in due course attain as near to God as is possible for any human being to do, and that he will preach the gospel of deliverance to the whole world." My father was overjoyed; he expressed his regret, and we became friends once more as before.

9

The Engine Refuses to move

I WENT to Poona and joined the Deccan College for my first LL.B. As usual I visited the various holy places on the way, and was very glad to see Narsoba Wadi, Audumbar and Kolhapur, the actual places where the miracles we read about in the *Guru-Charitra* were performed.

Narsoba Wadi is extremely beautiful. The sacred river Krishna is to be seen flowing there with all its majesty. There, too, are footprints of the Master worshipped by thousands of people. The desires of every pilgrim are fulfilled. Nobody goes away "empty-handed." Naturally very few came for spiritual illumination; those who did had sometimes to stay as long as forty years. All and sundry had their worldly difficulties, and they were tided over these. Everybody stays till, in a dream, the Master asks him to leave. Not a few come possessed by spirits, and as soon as they are brought into the temple, when the ceremony of Arati has been gone through, they scream and dance and weep. Then, questioned by the priests, the spirits proclaim their identity to the surprise of all. After the ceremony the pilgrims have to dip in the sacred river, and are free from any trouble in future. The most wonderful thing was that each spirit gave a reason why it had taken possession of the body, and was always willing to leave it at the bidding of the Master. Though I had not come there with my petition, yet like almost everybody who goes to this place, I was proud to beg for my food, which is the penance appointed to win favour from the Master, whether for prince or pauper.

I met some sadhus and swamis, and discussed with them whenever this was possible. I saw a remarkable woman singer there. She was clad in a snow-white garment, and played with one hand upon the *veena*, a stringed instrument, while marking time with the other

The Engine Refuses to move

on the *tabla*, a small drum, and singing in an exceedingly sweet voice the praises of the Divine Master. Hers was a beautiful story. She was born of the family of Naikins, the professional singers and courtesans. Her mother was very wealthy, and her lover, or can we say her husband, was immensely wealthy. These singers are generally attached to one person and observe very strict rules of chastity. They are not prostitutes of the ordinary type.

She was suffering from some disease and had spent thousands of rupees for the best medical help, but to no purpose. At last she came to Narsoba Wadi and regained her health. After a month she yielded to the persuasion of her husband and started for home, but as soon as she was beyond the limits of the village, she felt her malady return. She retraced her steps, and again left, and again had to return. So long as she was there, she was well. At last she was tired of setting out and coming back, and consulted the great Shri Tembe Swami.[1] The Swamiji told her that there was no remedy but to stay. It was impossible for her to go away, since it was not the will of the Divine Master, for she had desired illumination and not merely health and life at home. Ultimately she bade good-bye to her mother, her husband and her property, and lived there, and sang all the while the glory of the Divine Master. She begged her food and was practising yoga as instructed by the Swamiji. She was extremely beautiful, clad in her white *sari*, and singing in her sweet voice. I was enchanted and sat near her to enjoy her singing as long as possible.

I went to Hubli and wanted to pay my respects to the Shri Siddharudha Swami, but was told that he never came out of his room till 3 P.M., and my train back was at 2 P.M. His disciples tried to persuade me that it was useless to wait, but I said: "I can afford to sit here till 1 P.M. No matter whether the Swami comes forth or not; to wait for him will be a penance." At five minutes to one I was preparing to leave, when to the surprise of all he came out of his room and directly to me. After my salutation was over, he spoke in very mild tones: "My child, God bless you. You need not be disheartened, though it is a long and tedious process. The Master

---

[1] A Shrine to honour Tembe Swami was built just behind and above the temple after his death. *Editor.*

will help you. Have faith in Him, and everything will be accomplished in proper time. Meanwhile, control yourself if you want to know yourself." He gave me his benediction, accepted my salutation, and went away after throwing another loving glance at me. The joy I felt at that meeting can better be imagined than described.

I met many swamis who belonged to the lesser fry, but I gleaned something or other from each. I had discovered the right attitude of mind, and reaped a good harvest.

At Kalyan I joined the High School as a teacher, going to Bombay every evening to keep up terms for the final LL.B. I was very busy with work in the school, in the gymnasium, in the law class, and at night I was practising the first steps in the path of yoga. I lived on milk and fruit only, which helped to keep my mind pure, as I knew that mind is the product of the food we eat, therefore the purer the food, the purer our minds are bound to become. I made the experiment, and found this to be the fact.

The nights were very happy, for I passed them in meditation. I came from Bombay after 10 P.M., had my bath, and began to meditate on Lord Dattatreya, and to repeat the Gayatri mantra to myself: "We meditate on the supreme splendour of the Divine Being; may it illuminate our intellects." I felt refreshed while my mind slowly gathered peace in silence. It was physical and mental purification; the milk diet helped the one, and the Gayatri mantra helped the other. I also practised the various postures of yoga, and they contributed immensely to the process of concentration. Besides, I consistently observed the various rules and regulations prescribed for a student by Bhagwan Patanjali, keeping vows of harmlessness, truth-speaking, continence, purity, contentment, austerity, reading the scriptures, devotion to God. I was very fond of Siddhasana, the posture of the adepts. As regards breathing exercises, I did not practise of any, having more faith in the natural processes Raja-Yoga (control of the mind) than those of Hatha-Yoga. Breathing exercises ought only to be performed under the guidance of an expert master; for the slightest mistake may set up various kinds of malady. I firmly believed that by meditation an automatic process would silently develop and lead me on to Pranayam or the control of *prana*, the source of vital energy in man. At the same time I tried to wean my senses from their various

3. Temple at Narsoba Wadi on the banks of Krishna.
(Photograph by Vinod Sena)

objects, for that was the fifth stage in yoga called the **Pratyahara**. I was a convinced student, who always believed in what he did. Having seen so many practical illustrations of yogic powers, I should have been the greatest fool on earth had I not believed in them. But the question before me was not faith, but actual experience. Faith carried me to a certain point, but when my patience began to tire, actual experience came to my aid, and thus I could successfully combat the various difficulties that stood in the way, and attain the stage which I have attained today, whatever its value may be.

One day I read in the newspapers that some sadhus made a public demonstration of walking on live fire. Not only did they walk over it, but enabled laymen to do the same with impurity. Wonderful, nay, marvellous! The English people talked about the event, discussed it publicly and privately, without knowing what power lay behind the phenomena, which was Agni-Stambhan and Jala-Stambhan, or the control of fire and water which result from the repetition of certain mantrams or spells.

A still more wonderful miracle was in store for Bombay (vide, newspapers for 1906). One day a sadhu, or holy man, went to the railway station and requested the ticket collector to admit him to the train, saying he was a sadhu and had no money for a ticket. The Anglo-Indian[1] not only did not listen to his request, but pushed him aside rudely. He took the insult very calmly and muttered to himself: "I will see now whether this train will start." The driver whistled, and tried to start the train, but to no purpose. The engine refused to obey. Others came to help, all failed. The train service was very frequent, and as the first train could not start, many others were held up. Wires were sent to the head office. Experts arrived; they tried their best, all to no avail. For one full hour the service was at a standstill. Ultimately the Indian stationmaster, who knew that the sadhu had intervened, approached the officials and said to them: "Unless that sadhu who is standing outside the gate is given a seat in the train, it is not likely to start." He was ridiculed, but after a short time common sense prevailed, and the sadhu was accommodated comfortably in a first-class compartment, and the train

---

[1] "Anglo-Indian" is now the legal substitute for the old term "Eurasian."

steamed off. It was a practical demonstration, and the officials, however wise, had to climb down. Thenceforth the sadhu was allowed to travel first class.

I had read books in which the various mantrams by which these results were obtained appeared. Somewhat later I even practised repeating one among them that controlled prosperity. When this outstanding miracle became the talk of Bombay and the commonest souls were the most impressed by it, I felt a strong revulsion and realised as never before that, weighed against spiritual values, such power was of small account. Had not the Yogi Shri Ramdas Swami[1] been called by simple folk to come and see a sadhu who was walking across the river Krishna, and when he saw it remarked:, "This is a wonderful feat indeed, and when one comes to think of it worth exactly one half penny, for which sum the ferryman would have taken the sadhu across." So was the power to prevent the engine from starting worth exactly the fare to the sadhu's destination.

As the saying goes in Marathi: "When you shut the nose, the mouth opens." Here at least the mouth opened. And everywhere they talked about the incident, and College students, carried away with patriotism, said: "Tell the Englishmen in England that all their machine-guns and warships are only able to work so long as a Mahatma does not will otherwise. India is the land of the Mahatmas—beware of them!" But "Does this talk help them towards realisation of the Divine?" was my thought, since I was striving more and more for Bhakti Yoga (union with God through the love of Him), and I knew that I was tempted by a lower aim when asked to admire the powers displayed in such feats.

[1] See *supra*, p. 20.

10

May Shri Gurudeo Bless You!

MY parents recognised whither the current of my life was setting, and were afraid that I might quit home at any time. My father studied astrology himself in order to test the predictions of the various astrologers and discovered that it was my fate to travel in search of illumination. With all his seriousness, he was fondly attached to me. My mother tried to coax me to stay within the bounds prescribed by her affection, but I was growing fast, and her affection was not strong enough to allay the thirst for the divine love. They wanted me to marry; they thought that would tie me to the home; but I refused. Whenever I went to Amraoti, they tried to feed me with rich dishes, but I refused everything except fruit and milk.

I ever kept the softest corner in my heart for them, and was ready to sacrifice my principles for their sake. How much I owed them in life, and obedience was written in my heart. My father was fast losing all faith in the worldly life. He had centered all his hopes in me, and that I was to go away he was now certain. He spent much of his time in reading the sacred scriptures and the lives of the great Mahatmas. This gave him a great consolation. Every now and then he visited the shrines of the saints, and tried to serve them and win spiritual illumination. My attitude towards life opened his eyes to the fact that a cruel experiment would be made in his own house. He knew that there was nothing in me about which he could feel ashamed, but on the contrary everything to be proud of. In fact, many a time he took me with him to visit saints, and was very glad to see that they welcomed me with both arms.

My mother caressed me in public, but when alone she wept in silence. She had brought me up with ideas and ambitions of her own, and when she found they were being thwarted, she naturally felt very much depressed. Her extreme attachment for me was at the root of all her misery. She became day by day more and more unhappy, prayed to all the gods to keep me in the home, and as she was extremely sincere, her prayers were granted, but only temporarily.

I tried to control myself, and succeeded by the Grace of God. I had become desperate, but thank Heaven there was improvement. Slowly but surely my mind submitted itself to my persuasion, and I was again able to move in society with a clean conscience. This was a great triumph for me. There were temptations, many and various, at every step, but I was quite impervious. I had youth, beauty and charm, learning and money, and naturally needed to be always wide awake. Frequently I was saved only just in time by recalling the couplet of Bharavi, the great Sanskrit poet. His ear was so delighted with it that he ran immediately into the market and announced that he had a poem for sale. People asked: "What is your price?" He said: "A lakh of rupees" (i.e., seven thousand pounds). "How long is it?" "Two lines." This provoked jeers and laughter. However, one very rich merchant paid the price, for he said: "Bharavi is a very great poet", and later had the precious words copied in letters of gold on the door of his best room. No translation can render their music, barely their sense:

Never act rashly, for rashness lets in a
host of calamities.

Not long after the merchant's business led him to Baghdad and Cairo, and sixteen years were gone before he returned home. He was about to enter his wife's apartment when he heard talking within and, listening, recognised a young man's voice as well as hers. Muttering to himself: "Was I mistaken in her? Has she deceived me?" he drew his sword, when suddenly his eye caught the words of gold and he let the blade slip back in the scabbard, then entered the room. His wife ran to meet him with exclamation of joy, and when she had kissed his feet, called to her companion: "Come and worship your father whom we have mourned these many years!" "Golden words indeed," the merchant would say, retelling the story. "They were cheap indeed, at a lakh of rupees."

4. Hamsa Swami as a young sanyasin,
photo kept by Purohit Swami during his travels.

May Shri Gurudeo Bless You!

I too had been born and bred in sentiment. But I knew that however pure the sentiment might be, it was a source of weakness. I wanted to control my passions, and with my success my strength increased. Self-control is the basis of all power.

Shri Narayen Maharaj of Kedgaon came to Bombay. Thousands of people flocked to see him. Special trains were run, in order to relieve the congestion. On Sunday generally the service was slow and far between, and they found it very difficult to cope with the crowds. He stayed with a courtesan. Thousands went to have a sight of him at her house. It became a sacred place of pilgrimage, and ultimately developed into an ashram, the monastery of the saint.

He spoke very little, was humble and courteous, and wrought many a miracle. Some Englishmen took a great fancy to him. Many went to him merely to ridicule, but remained there to pray. Most admired and worshipped, some heaped ridicule on him; but neither could dislodge him from his peace. That was the greatest miracle he performed.

I remember when I went to pay my respects to him, one of the High Court Pleaders of Bombay was there. He was disgustingly drunk. The devotees were singing the praises of the Lord. The pleader was belching the fumes of his drink. Some people felt sick, but the Maharaj was all kindness to him. All of a sudden the pleader vomited, and everybody felt disgusted except the Maharaj, whose garments were spoiled. He loved him but the more, gave him his blessing, and today he is one of his best disciples. This was an example of the practical good that the saints can do, and impressed me very much. People found fault with him because he stayed with the courtesan, but should have praised him the more; for to a saint human beings are equals, whether they be paragons of virtue or the lowest prostitutes. There is nothing despicable in this world for a Mahatma, and he never shuns a thing because it is not good in the eyes of the world, nor embraces any because the world honours it. He ought to be above good and evil.

My visions were now all beautiful. They gave consolation to my feverish mind. Hanuman, the god of strength; Shiva, the god who frequents those grounds where the bodies of the dead are burned, appeared to me in sleep. I was slowly drifting towards the worship of Lord Dattatreya. When he came I knew that he was the god whom I worshipped pre-eminently. Then the great truth dawned upon me that all gods are one. My worship changed with my psychology. But the truth remained that God, in whatever form you worship him, is willing to manifest himself according to the wishes of the devotee. Men find the good they seek with pure love.

The various gods in India have their special attributes in addition to the attributes of divine perfection. Every man is free to worship the God who suits his individual psychology, and that is for him the most perfect way of approaching divinity. Some lay more stress on one divine form, some on another, but when they realise one they realise all, though they may still prefer to contemplate the God who helped them to realisation. I was to find out the unity of all gods by the help of Lord Dattatreya, on whom ever since my attention has rested.

Already then, when I was at work or in the street, I repeated his name to myself. Everyday I grew more serious, and restless at the same time. I longed to leave home and parents, and run to the Himalayas in search of Him. But better counsel prevailed. Where was the use of going to the Himalayas unless I made myself spiritually able to stay there? So many went to the Himalayas and came back empty. I must advance in meditation before I contemplated going. My conviction always had been that once you take a forward step you should never, never go back.

One day, lying on my grass mat with my hand as my pillow, I wept, and wept. I thought that my Master was cruel, but a second thought followed immediately, declaring that I was not deserving. I said to myself, desert should precede desire. Yes, that was true.

All of a sudden there was a tap at the door. A College friend of mine came in. He saw that my eyes were sore with weeping. He asked me the reason. I was silent. He guessed it and suggested that we should both go to a Mahatma, who was at Dadar and who was his personal friend.[1] I was willing, and off we started.

We ascended the stairs in the Keertikar's building, and were admitted into a small room on the top floor. As I entered, the Swami who was sitting on a tiger's skin rose, our eyes met, and I flew to meet him, and he fondly clasped me in his arms. What a great bliss it was to be in the arms of that great blessed soul! It was the purest form of bliss that I had ever enjoyed.

[1] Shri Natekar (1878-1937). On being initiated into the Giri Order of Swamis on Mount Kailash, he assumed the name of Hamsa Swami. *Editor.*

May Shri Gurudeo Bless You!

Our common friend, who introduced me to the Swami, was dumbfounded when he saw how familiar we were with each other. That was love at first sight. It was pure divine love, and it shines today in the hearts of both as it did on that first day. The Swami, while still embracing me, said softly, with music in his voice: "We meet again after such a long time!" Yes, he was right, we had known each other in past incarnations. He knew it, I did not. But he was right. He offered me a seat and we talked, and my friend wondered to see us so free and easy. The Swami had just come out of his meditation. His eyes sparkled with that divine love which he had realised. His body was quite warm, and I felt the warmth of his heart in my embrace. He was very lean, without a pound of flesh on his body, but his face gleamed with ecstasy. He had more beautiful features than I had ever beheld, and his soul, in proof, surpassed them. His voice was so sweet, it was worthy of a yogi. For yogi means yoked with God, that is, one who has so controlled his mind as to render it both open and obedient to divine influence. The word derives from *yuja*, to join. His breath was full of perfume and sent a thrill through my veins.

That was the first time when I was lost in the embrace of a Mahatma. I shall never forget the inexplicable joy felt at that time. We talked in plain, simple language. I revealed the anguish of my heart. He gave me his blessing and asked me not to be anxious, as my Master was there to take care of me. "Really, is it a fact that my Master wants me?" I asked him. "Yes," was the emphatic reply. "Though you do not know Him, He knows you. Though you are not in a position to appreciate Him, yet a day will come when you will. Never be anxious. Love Him, and you shall realise Him."

We rose, and again he offered to embrace me. I flew to him. I remember I shed some hot tears. We remained in that state for a few minutes. Then he released his embrace very gently, placed his palm on my head, and said: "May Shri Gurudeo bless you!"

11

Come to Me!

THE Mahatmas showed me the way, yet day by day I grew more desperate, though impatience is no help where the utmost patience is required. I wanted to grasp the moon, but she was a long way off. The path chalked out for me must be followed before light would automatically increase. I tried to persuade myself to the belief that spirituality was a slow and steady growth, that no Master, however competent, could carry me on his shoulders. Let me not act as a helpless child, but fight my way as a brave soldier. Still the heart leaped up, only to find that the light was not only not nearer, but far, far away—an excruciating pain to undergo!

I was usually gay and cheerful, but at times seriousness ended in sadness. This annoyed me very much. Somehow I was not acting in the right way, but tried to weigh my physical and mental strength against the goal to be reached, and then adjust my conduct. No conduct must precede, that was the first lesson in introspection or self-examination, as we may call it. Henceforward everything should be regular. I would meditate for a fixed period and no more. What was the good of my meditating for a longer time, and enjoying it, if a reaction set in the next day. Everything, even meditation, under control was the true order of life. I increased the period very slowly, one minute every alternate day. I used to get up early in the morning, at 5 A.M., but it took many months before I could rise at 3 A.M. I was very slow, but determined never to retrace a single step. The result of being carried away by sentiment was that you grew weaker and weaker. Strength was necessary, and slow and steady self-control was the way to obtain it.

I wandered from place to place in search of light. I read many books on religion and yoga. At last one day the crisis came. I was reading the *Geeta*, the gospel of Lord Shrikrishna. "Passion, anger and avarice are the three great enemies. Therefore kill them." Such precepts, though read every day, seemed useless. They must be realised. Study only made me more intellectual. My need was not for knowledge, but for wisdom. Learning could not give me control. My soul was sick and was not helped by medicine administered to the intellect, since they were two separate things. I must prescribe for my soul; success in self-control, that would cure it. This plain and simple philosophy appealed to me.

I threw away all the sacred books, including the *Geeta*, and sat down to contemplate and meditate on Lord Dattatreya, with all the forces of my mind that I could command. I looked at His divine form with steady eyes. I repeated His name constantly and read regularly the *Avadhoota Geeta*,[1] the gospel preached by Him to his first and favourite disciple, Shri Kartikeya Swami. I reduced all my spiritual activities to the simple formula given above and determined to visit no more places of pilgrimage nor Mahatmas. These latter had given me their advice, my duty was to embody it in practice.

A great change was wrought in me. I no longer liked discussing questions of spirituality. Keen debater though I had been, my friends were now told that my faith in discussions was superseded. They called me a "fool" and a "crank." They could not realise that he who ascends a ladder has to leave rung after rung behind him. To see Mahatmas was not the aim of my life, but only a means; yet when I refused to visit any more Mahatmas, my friends were surprised. I told them: "My refusal does not imply any disrespect, but only proves that I am bent on realising what they have taught me. If I went again, they could only repeat precepts which were better honoured should I practise them." My friends seldom understood this; they accused me of self-sufficiency. Soon they left me severely alone, much to my gain. So long as you conform to the ideas of your friends, they remain, but so soon as there arise differences of opinion and conduct, they fall off and begin to

---

[1] Purohit Swami's last years were spent in polishing his English rendering of the work. It was published posthumously by the publisher of the present book in 1979 with an Introduction by S. Mokashi-Punekar. *Editor.*

ridicule. I had to pay for a right understanding of human nature. Though in the beginning shocked, yet by and by custom hardened me, and after a certain time there was nothing in this world over which I would allow myself to feel surprise.

I was at Amraoti staying with my parents. All of a sudden a call came from a friend at Nagpur. He wrote to my father and requested him to send me at once, as he had a Mahatma with him as a guest. I had to obey and went to Nagpur. The Mahatma treated me very kindly. He was very tall and looked very gay and happy. He had a long white beard that added grace to his beautiful face. He was blind of both eyes and, as the story went, "had blown away his eyes", saying that he saw all that was worth seeing without them. I soon found that he had developed his inner sight so well that the loss of his eyes was not felt.

He talked freely to me and tested me in various ways. I served him as faithfully as I could. He was so pleased that he offered to teach me the art of alchemy, but I refused to learn, telling him that alchemy would give me worldly goods which I had never sought for. My need was God, and God alone. He was extremely pleased, for many harassed him begging to be taught alchemy, but he refused. One day he said: "These worldly people want to exploit this great yogi art for their own selfish ends. They shall not do it. It is intended alone for those at one with God."

I was seriously thinking of giving up my law course, because I thought it would mean wasted time, money and energy; but the Mahatma insisted on my appearing for the final LL.B. I told him that I should never practise in the courts, and that it would be of no use to me. But he persisted and wrung a promise from me. Though there were only three months left, he told me he took the responsibility of seeing to it that I passed. I had to obey.

I went to Bombay, filled up the form, paid the University fees, came to Amraoti, studied for three months at an average of seven and a half hours every day, and appeared for the examination. It cost no end of tedious pains to wade through all those intricate problems of law, but faith and self-control helped me.

When I was studying one day, Lord Dattatreya manifested Himself in a dream under the form in which I was worshipping Him. I saluted Him, and He said to me with a sweet smile on His

Come to Me!

lips: "My beloved child, why are you wandering hither and thither? Come to me?" and He disappeared. This seemed like a direct call, but I was afraid to think so, since the idea was very ambitious and my deserts seemed far from correspondent.

After the last paper was given in, I went to Dadar to my friend in the evening, and we were so glad to meet. There were no secrets between us. He was leaving for Mount Girnar, the sacred place where the footprints of Lord Dattatreya are, and he was willing to take me with him. I was delighted. Mount Girnar was the sacred seat of the Lord, and many yogis in Maharashtra had had sight of Him there. This was the dream of my life, and made me very impatient.

My reader may perhaps say, "Why do you not give your friend's name?" I answer: "My friend has become my Master and has given his name into his disciple's keeping. If in future I should not add honour to it by what I say and do, misery would be mine. The day will come when what I have done will be evident, then mine will be joined with his in glory, or separated from it by being forgotten for ever. Till then my pen withholds it instinctively."

The next morning we both started at 7.30 from Grant Road, and reached Junagad the day after at 5 P.M. In the distance I saw the mountain, and saluted my Divine Master, the Master of all Masters, as He is called by the yogis.

12

Practise Penance

THIRTY-FOUR hours' railway journey with changes at Viramgaon, Dhola and Jetalsar. The nights were bitterly cold, and the wind was blowing fiercely against us. We sat like statues of youth, facing each other; my friend, only four years the older, seemed to shine with an inner light, but had scarcely any flesh on him. I too was buoyant though immensely bulky. Many wondered who we were, and it must have been evident that we were of good family and sincere in our religion. My friend wore a gown of orange, and I as his attendant waited on him. Neither of us ate or drank anything throughout the journey. We were frequently offered food, milk and fruits, but everything was courteously refused. As soon as the peaks of Mount Girnar came into sight, we got down, knelt, folded our hands, and saluted the Lord Dattatreya.

We were received at Junagad station by Mr. M.M. Joshi, Professor of Sanskrit at the Bahuddin College. We took a bath, then sat in meditation for a couple of hours, when, after saying grace, my friend ate rice and bread, while I fared on milk and fruit as usual.

Our daily rule was to rise at 3 A.M. and begin our meditation at four, both sitting in the same room on a grass mat over which a white blanket was spread, and over that a tiger-skin with a white garment to cover all. This made a most comfortable seat. A photograph of the Lord's picture stood in front of us among sweet-smelling flowers, and incense was burning. The whole atmosphere was spiritually intoxicating. We finished our meditation at ten, and had our lunch. Again at noon we had a second bath, and went into meditation until 4 P.M. Then we chatted together before our third bath at sunset, after which we meditated till 9 P.M., when dinner was served. I took not more than a pound of milk and some watery fruit throughout the day. People came to see us, and were curious to find out which of us was the superior. Their judgment was invariably at fault. I pitied them.

The fighting spirit was still within me and I tried to argue. Everybody without exception blamed me for pursuing the spiritual life, when my duty was to stay with my parents and serve them. How could they understand the pangs of my heart? At last I found it was futile to argue, being too old an oak to bend, and they also were in the same case. So I obeyed the sage Narada's aphorism of "Vain discussions are to be avoided."

For nearly three weeks our daily routine remained the same. I in fact starved myself, but did not feel any depression. They were the happiest days of my life. I sat alone with my friend and talked about the great spiritual truths, frequently obtaining glimpses of the means by which he had come so near to realisation. Terrible were the sacrifices that he had made, but they had successfully built up intimate relations with the Lord; he talked with Him, meditated on His form, repeated His name, and consulted Him, in fact his whole life was under His direction. Even about worldly matters he waited for the Lord's lead like a most obedient disciple. I had loved him when we first met at Bombay; now my love increased hourly. When he was absent, I felt the separation so keenly as to astonish myself. My grandmother had had the keys of my affection when I was a child; then my mother; but now a new era began to dawn as, unconsciously, I handed them over to my best-beloved friend, guide, philosopher and Master; yet I did not know then that he was destined to become my Master.

The anniversary day of the birth of the Lord Dattatreya fell on the 25th December 1907. We both rose early in the morning, had our bath, and set out for Mount Girnar. The moon was shining, and we had to walk three miles to reach the foot of the mountain. We repeated to ourselves the name of the Lord. The morning was very beautiful. Birds began to sing the song of freedom, everywhere priests in the temples chanted praises and burnt incense to the Lord. The whole scene was pervaded with joyous piety.

There are nearly 7,000 beautifully built steps of granite. After a few hundred I grew tired. I had had very little nourishment for the last three weeks, and found the ascension taxing. My friend cheered me. Hundreds of pilgrims were climbing, and I felt ashamed that I

5. The Dattatreya Peak of Mount Girnar (Photograph by Vinod Sena).

Practise Penance

could not ascend more quickly. I needed a rest after each hundred steps, which meant great delay. We must reach the peak, where the sacred footprints are impressed on a stone slab, before evening. I had doubts as to whether it would prove physically possible.

We were very courteously treated by the sadhus and the pilgrims. I refused to take either milk or fruit by the way and only drank water from time to time. My friend sang the glory of the Master whenever I sat for rest under the shade of a tree, and would try to find and bring water to me. We came to the Gomukhi Kund at midday. The beautiful tank had a thin crust of ice on it. The wind was fierce; the sun was bright; the ascent exhausting. We entered the temple of the Lord Shiva, and I stretched myself out at full length for a while, before going to my bath in the waters of the pool. How marvellously refreshing that bath was!

On the edge of the pool I was still worshipping the Lord, and repeating the Upanishads, when all of a sudden I saw a beautiful form, leaning against the trunk of an audumbar tree; with a wonderful, fascinating smile she beckoned me to her. I was dumbfounded. Her oval face, her dark and shining eyes, her red lips were so lovely, and her gesture so irresistible. I ran to her. She was a yogini. I fell at her feet; she raised me up, and with a soft gleam in her eyes, said: "My beloved child, you are well met here; by the Grace of your Master, all your desires will be fulfilled. Have courage, do not be disheartened. Remember always that the Master's power is there to fall back on."

She placed the palms of her hands on my head and said, "May the Master bless you!" then gently asked me to leave her. I was so unwilling as to feel nailed to the ground. I yearned to speak, at least let me ask her name. But no. Something in her eyes told me that no question was permitted. With bitter disappointment I felt forced to leave her, but after a few paces was bold enough to look back. Nobody was there. Could I have dreamed? The yogini had disappeared. She had done her duty, given me a message, why should she stay? But how could she disappear so suddenly? That was more than I could tell.

My friend only gave me a sweet and silent smile when told about her.

We reached the Ambaji Hill, then the Gorakhanath Hill, from which we could see the Dattatreya Hill. We prostrated ourselves on the pavement when we caught sight of the orange flag floating over it, and I prayed to my Master that I might reach the summit before evening. Every moment made me more desperate. We climbed down the hill we were on, then up the steps that rose over against it. The evening was closing round. The sun was setting beneath the horizon. I summoned my last strength, and with a great effort reached the slab and fell prostrate over the sacred footprints.

I do not know what happened after that. When I came to my senses, I found I was profusely perspiring, and my friend had laid my head on his lap and was pouring water in at my mouth. I tried to get up, but was so weak that I fell back again. My friend sprinkled some water on my head, applied it to my eyes and forehead, and I came to my senses again. The full moon was shining bright in the sky. The wind was ferocious, the cold extremely biting.

My friend asked me: "Are you satisfied?"

"Yes, by the grace of the Divine Master, I am. I know not when or where, but I saw Him, in that same form on which I meditate, and He said: 'Come to me, my beloved child! Where are you roaming? Practise penance, and you shall find me.'"

I remembered I had been so desperate earlier in the day as to resolve on throwing myself from the cliff should I not hear any message. But He had spoken and given me consolation and guidance at least. I prayed and wept, and came down slowly but with a firm step, and was at the bottom of the hill by ten. We hired a carriage and came to Mr. Joshi's place at eleven, where we had our baths, took our milk, said our prayers, and, with the sacred name of the Lord on our lips, went to rest. I was very happy to have been accepted, and my friend was extremely glad. He corroborated my vision. The aim of my life had seemed so distant, but here was a beginning made towards its fulfilment.

By whom had I been accepted? I will now tell my reader a little of what I then knew about the Lord Dattatreya, in whom Lord Brahma-deo the creator, Lord Vishnu the preserver, and Lord Shiva the destroyer are made one by incarnation. The story is told thus.

One day the sage Narada went to Mother Parvati, the wife of

Lord Shiva, and sang the praises of Anasooya as the most wonderful and chaste lady in the world. He then went to Mother Lakshmi, the wife of Lord Vishnu, and did the same thing. Thereupon they prevailed upon their husband-gods to go and see Anasooya, the wife of sage Atri, and to take with them Lord Brahma-deo, their celibate brother, and to put her to the test. The Lords Brahma-deo, Vishnu and Shiva came to the cottage when her husband was out in the forest. They begged her to serve them with food immediately, and she served them in her husband's name. Her serenity was unruffled even by the presence of the three most beautiful gods, and after the meal they asked her to beg a boon of them. She saluted, and said that being already blessed by their presence, she desired them to remain in her home permanently in the form of a child. They were forced by their oath to consent, and so all three took the form of the babe Dattatreya. The mother Anasooya nursed it, and her husband, the sage Atri, when he returned from the forest was overjoyed to see the gods in the form of his son.

Lord Dattatreya grew up and became the first yogi, the Master of all Masters as He is called in India. His mission is to give the knowledge of spiritual science to this world. He has blessed thousands of souls, and in the realm of spirituality He holds the first place. Even Lord Shrikrishna paid Him tribute of praise while talking to His disciple Shri Uddhava Swami. In Maharashtra especially He is highly worshipped. The Great Mahatmas are in touch with Him. He still wears diverse garbs, goes to Benares every morning for His bath, begs for His food at Kolhapur, holds His durbar on Mount Girnar, and goes to bed at Mount Mahur, and travels the world, doing His work of love and peace, and is seen by those who are initiated. He is known throughout India, but especially in the land of Mahrattas. His anniversary day is celebrated on the full moon, in the month of Marga-Sheersha, which generally coincides with December. People fast on Thursday as a sacred day in His honour, and in such big towns as Bombay flowers are sold at double the price on the day dedicated to Lord Dattatreya.

Thousands of people have visions of Him. He every now and then incarnates in new forms. The followers of Shiva and Vishnu worship Him as incarnations of them. The yogis worship Him as the Master Yogi; the Jains worship Him as the Neminath, and even the Moslems worship Him as the Great Fakir. I have come across many a Mohammedan fakir who had a special devotion for Him. He is above all caste and creed and religion, for His is the mission of Love and Peace and divine union. The picture of Him which helps my worship has also a wonderful story. The artist Bhat lived at Wai about thirty-five years ago and had prayed for a vision of the Lord so that he might portray Him. After a number of years the prayer was answered, but under very curious circumstances. The artist was attacked by plague, and that same night he saw the vision. He at once got up, took his brushes and set to work. Whenever the vision faded, he closed his eyes and it returned. He worked for three days and nights, in spite of a very high temperature, without any food, and when he laid down his brush, he shut his eyes, wept tears of gratitude, sank on his bed, and breathed his last. But there stood the life-size oil painting, which is now at Bombay, of the Master whom he loved and worshipped. In India every activity, including the arts of singing, dancing and painting, is dedicated to a spiritual goal.

6. Lord Dattatreya, after Bhat's painting
This picture along with his guru's was carried by the author wherever he went.

13

God and Mammon

I WAS beaming with joy, for I was definitely accepted by the Master of all Masters, though not as a disciple, yet as a servant. I must strive hard to deserve to be a disciple, but first I wanted to serve and wished to see my service accepted, however humble and wayward it might be.

The next morning came the news that I had passed my LL.B. The degree had no charm for me, for I did not mean to cash it in the law courts, but it made me extremely glad that the prophecy of that blind sage had come true. Our friends at Junagad bored me with questions as to where and when I should practise, but I maintained silence. Had I confessed that money-making had no attraction for me, they would have taken it for a joke.

My friend was the only person on earth who completely sympathised with my spiritual ambitions. He had had his share of ridicule already, and he gave me the strength to undergo the censure that was heaped upon me because I aspired to a more perfect rule of life. My friend told me that he was ordered to go to Mount Kailas, and that he would be leaving very shortly. He was determined to have a sight of his Divine Master, Bhagwan Shri Dattatreya, the Lord of Trinity, or, failing that, he would leave his body in the Himalayas since he could brook the separation no longer. His body had become too delicate; it was always burning, at times it was very hot; his eyes sparkled with eagerness, and his mind was bent upon achieving the sole object of his life. He asked me to accompany him. I told him that I was not fit to do so, for to climb the Himalayas all the while thinking of your home would be but a physical gesture. I was mentally unfit to go. He accepted my refusal in good part, for he knew me better even than I knew myself, but told me that this might be our last meeting. He had an iron will, and I felt sure that the Lord would bless him and that I should see my most beloved friend, crowned with success, at no distant date. Oh how dearly I loved him! I could not imagine loving anybody more on this earth, yet I knew my love was nothing as compared with his for me.

I left Junagad for Amraoti, and broke my journey at Nardhana, on the Tapti Valley railway. I hired a bullock-cart, and reached Songir at midnight. It was the month of January. The wind was blowing fiercely in my face, the cold was bitter, and there was not a human being to be seen, when I reached the cottage where Shri Boa Maharaj was staying. A small oil-lamp was burning in a corner, the Swami was sitting on a simple *charpai*, the fire was burning before him, and his faithful dog ran towards me and licked my hands.

I put off all my clothes, put a rag round my loins, had a bath in the tank and went towards the cottage, all the while repeating the name of my Master. I was shivering with cold. The Swami got up from his couch as I came forward, and muttered to himself as though directing servants: "Come along, come along, my child. Welcome to my palace. Hullo! get some milk for my child. Oh how hungry he feels! Get him some milk at once! He is extremely hungry." I fell at his feet. He asked me to get up, and went to his bed. I was sitting by the fireside and gradually getting warm. He talked on in his sweet voice. My hunger had vanished as much as if I had drunk the milk he had commanded to be brought me, and I felt that a wonderful peace entered into my mind. Mentally I asked him some questions, without uttering a word, and he answered them all. He talked on in his own fashion: "What is the use of that rag of a diploma! To earn money? Well, you can worship mammon, but be sure that you cannot worship God at the same time. Where is that wealth which your forefathers heaped up. Where are all those palanquin poles? They have all been used for firewood. What a tragedy! And still you want to earn money? What a beautiful body god has given you! I wonder whether it will be wasted on the service of mammon. It would give me more pleasure if it were spent on realising God. Think ten times before you make any decision."

Then he described how happy God had made him; how He had given him that palace, meaning his hut; how He had given him a beautiful bed to sit and lie on; how the fire was always kept burning to ward off the cold; how He inspired somebody to bring him his daily bread; how He loved him, and accepted his small love in return, and how He had sent his most faithful servant, meaning his dog, to keep company with him, and how, raised above want, he lived happy and cheerful. Then he repeated, as if in a dream, the name of his master Shri Gahininath Swami, until his eyes shone with a divine ecstasy which is only seen in saints of his type.

My petty desires still swayed me, and he asked me whether I wanted them to be fulfilled. I felt ashamed and replied in the negative; and told him that I never had intended to earn money, and wanted to realise God before anything else. He was delighted and begged me to be all eyes and walk warily and gave me his blessing. Then I took leave with a heavy heart.

I had not eaten anything throughout the day, but his words of love fed me. He asked his dog to see me off, and that honest servant followed me to my cart, licked my feet and hands, and, throwing a glance full of love at me, departed.

I went back to Nardhana station, and took the train for Akola wanted to pay my respects to Shri Gajanan Maharaja, who was lodged there. I entered into the ashram. There were choirs singing the glory of God, hundreds were coming in and going out, but the Swami was lying on a mattress covered all over with a beautiful Kashmere shawl. That morning he had never once looked at anybody. Folk came in, touched his feet with their foreheads, and went away. Nobody dared to ask him to open his eyes.

I entered to salute him, and whom should I see but my father Dadasahib, come to ask the Swami about my whereabouts. He had had no news of me, and naturally was extremely anxious. He was so glad to see me. I saluted him, and then the Swami.

I told my father about everything that had happened. He had been afraid that I had gone to the forest for good. We both wanted to leave by the evening train, and I sat at the feet of the Swami, silently praying that he might let us see him; especially I pleaded on behalf of my father whom I had made so miserable. The prayer was granted. The Swami all of a sudden took off his shawl, looked at us, and asked my father to go to the station and catch the train, and not to worry about me. He gave me his blessing and covered himself up as before. Everybody regarded us as unusually lucky.

God and Mammon

We reached Amraoti the same evening, and the happiness of my mother when she saw me knew no bounds. We talked, and the night ended before our talk. My friends everywhere questioned me about legal practice and money. I was sick of the subject. My father was more keen about me than about money, and he always discouraged them. How glad I was that at least one soul was spiritually inclined!

I had lost weight at Mount Girnar, but this was more than made good by the care of my mother. I could not refuse her entreaties; was she not my mother, my goddess? With the memory of Mount Girnar in my heart, I moved like a free bird. The post of Extra Assistant Commissioner was offered me with a salary that made our friends envy me. However, my father refused on my behalf. He told the Commissioner that he had served the Government as a slave; that was enough, he would never advise his son to do the same. Our friends counselled in vain; he was adamant, and I was with him.

To busy myself with spiritual life once more and escape from observation, I tried to discover Mahatmas to serve them, and learn from them. Dry books interested me no longer, but living books in the form of Mahatmas I consulted as opportunity offered. Some were very kind and spoke in plain terms, others preferred to use speech mystically. The great question to be faced was whether I should renounce everything at once, or settle down as a householder and marry according to the will of my parents, and earn money. Many advisers and wellwishers told me that the best way was to do both these things at the same time. But I felt that to serve mammon and God at the same time would be like thrusting two swords into one scabbard. The wiseacres were so insistent that I thought the best way was to avoid them and be a pilgrim once more, to let my mind resolve its doubts while breathing fresh air.

My advisers had one virtue: their age; in that I had no chance of overtaking them. Age counts in this world, and I had to bow down my head in silence before it. And to extricate myself from a difficult situation, I started to Mount Mahur, where Lord Dattatreya takes His rest at night. Thus the story went, and I hoped to verify it, nay possibly to surprise Him there while fast asleep.

14

The God's Bed

I LEFT Amraoti for Yeotmal, stayed there for a couple of days to enjoy the company of some of my University friends, swallowed their advice and pocketed their ridicule in peace, but kept my precious secret to myself; then went to Mahagaon in a bullock-cart, where I enjoyed the hospitality of a landowner who lent me his bullock-cart to go to Mahur. Neither the slow pace nor the motion of the ox-cart suited me, so I decided to walk, which would have merit as a penance, and, having dismissed the carter with a tip, I wended on through the reserve forest.

A silk-bordered dhoti, silk coat and silk turban gave me the appearance of a well-to-do gentleman rather than of a pilgrim; besides I carried more than enough money. But money did not count in the dense forest. Those whom I met warned me not to go alone, for there was danger ahead. But I knew that the name of my Lord on my tongue was a sufficient safeguard. Was it not to be my passport throughout life? The more I repeated His name, the more it calmed me. What miracles that precious name has achieved for me! Saints have always praised the efficacy of His name, and here was an opportunity for me to realise the full significance of it. My faith in the true source of life had received rude shocks, occasioned by my University education; now it was high time that it should be revived, for l was disillusioned as to the powers of my intellect. Book learning had failed to give me satisfaction. Words had proved mere words for me.

I argued with myself vehemently, addressing my mind with every persuasion: "Oh my beloved mind! Listen to me. Let us be friends, not enemies. I must have peace at all costs. If thou art willing to make peace with me, good! Otherwise I shall have recourse to stringent measures. If thou wilt wander away from object to object without my permission, I shall resist and force thee to repeat the name of the Lord. Once my faith was in thee. Thou hast betrayed me. But another way is still open. Help me with all thy power to rely on the Divine alone."

Thus I argued and tried to tether my fickle mind to His name as to a picket. Of course at first it was always breaking loose, but I knew it had a vested interest in me that it would not willingly abandon. I knew it was of no use forcing the mind to accept a superior will on a sudden, for the reaction would be too great. I must proceed by slow steps. When I felt tired of repeating His holy name silently, I repeated it aloud; when that became wearisome, I repeated Sanskrit hymns, and when I had had enough of that too, I repeated His name in Marathi my vernacular language, and when that too failed I sat down on a big slab of stone, or climbed a tree, and began to listen to the songs of the birds and admire the natural scenes that were around me. The worship of Nature relieved the worship of the spirit, and when that too failed, I would lie down comfortably on the grass, shut my eyes, and was fast asleep the next moment. When I got up, I took a bath, performed my worship and began to walk again.

I walked on for two days without any food. The villagers were reserving the whole milk for the calves, so had none to give. From one house only I got a glassful, which had, as the old lady told me when I had drunk it, been put aside for the child.

When I traversed the jungle, the inmost recesses of my heart were quaking, but I employed all my energies in trying to gather as much courage as possible. It was a transition period. I had been accumulating courage little by little, and with such success that all fear vanished.

I approached a small temple on the evening of the second day at the foot of a hill. I was over-tired and needed a night's rest. As I entered the door, an old man, with a spotless white beard, descended the steps. He saw me, stopped, looked very intently at me, and became serious. I saluted him, and asked him in my boyish simplicity if he would show me the place where the Lord Dattatreya slept. He smiled and said: "Come along, my friend. You are in the very place where the Lord takes His rest every night."

The old man took me by the hand and led me to his room in the temple-yard. He told me that he was the priest and had been in that place for the last twenty-five years or more. Harassed by the neighbours, he was on the point of leaving many a time in disgust, but always a message can e from Lord Dattatreya to this effect: "What is the use of leaving me and going somewhere else?" He added with a gleam in his eyes: "The Lord is merciful to me. He guards me always, insignificant creature though I am. I gave up everything for His sake when my hair was black. Now it has turned white, it is too late to change." And he turned round and said: "Can you believe that He told me in a vision the other night that his beloved child was to come, and that I was to take care of him. I was anxiously waiting for you, and here you are. Regard mine as your home. You are a thousand times welcome. But now let us go," he added, "and have a bath. It is time for the evening worship, and we must hasten, for as the evening shades deepen there is danger of meeting a leopard there, who is only too fond of associating with men."

And off we went, and hurriedly took our bath; then with a wet towel round my waist, I offered my prayers and went into the temple with the priest. It is a fine temple, built of stone, consisting of a narthex four times as large as the shrine. There in a corner was the couch on which the Lord was said to take His rest. The incense was burning, the priest chanted the Vedas in a sweet voice, and I helped him. We rang the bells and carried the sacred lights through the whole place, and offered sweet dishes and put up a prayer that the Lord would take His rest there that night. The bed was then made with snow-white sheets, soft pillows, and a Kashmere shawl over the whole. The pillows were anointed with attar of roses; the joss-sticks were burnt, and we knelt down and prayed a last prayer, then the venerable priest took my hand and said: "Dear boy, this is the place that you wanted to see. The Lord comes here every night. You may be lucky enough to see Him. I cannot say. But believe me, He always comes."

The God's Bed

I asked the priest when the Lord might be expected, and he answered: "Generally He comes after eleven. Perhaps you may hear the music made by His golden pattens and feel His presence pass, or you may see Him set out for Benares for his daily bath at three in the morning in the Ganges. He is so merciful, He may show you some favour. I cannot say." And he locked the bedroom door and took away the key.

He tried to persuade me to share his meal, but I refused. He brought me some milk, and that was enough. We talked on spiritual themes, of which he had wonderful tales to unfold. I found that his whole life had been dedicated to the Lord, and he was glad to describe many wonderful incidents in which the Lord had guarded him.

He had prepared a bed for me, but I requested him to allow me to stay just outside the temple, for I was anxious to see and know. The narthex was a big one, flagged with stone. I felt very cold, but wanted to watch. Seated on a towel with a *koupin* round my loins, I repeated the holy name, that I might obtain a direct experience. All was pitch dark. I listened to my breath, which at times seemed strangely heavy. Making neither sound nor movement through dread of losing my opportunity, even the silent repetition of the holy name seemed a disturbance. All my senses and mind were concentrated on the desire of seeing the Divine Master.

I had entered the hall at nine. Hours rolled on. I believe it was approximately one when I heard the beautiful music of the measured steps enter the hall. All of a sudden there was a gush of sweet perfume, and automatically I rose to greet Him, with my hands folded. I saluted again and again. My hair stood on end. I perspired profusely. Tears of gratitude rushed to my eyes. I had stood in prayer for a couple of hours at least when again I heard the music of the pattens and felt the Master pass out. I was quite sure that He had come, taken His rest, and gone. I was extremely elated.

Another hour, and the priest came with a lantern in his hand to see whether I was willing to take a bath. He found me sitting on the floor with folded hands. "Did you see anything?" he asked me. I gave the full description of what I heard and felt. He was overjoyed.

On the second night I sat once more in the hall praying. All of a sudden the tapping of the pattens was there, followed by a gush of sweet perfume, and a knock at the door of the temple room, as if somebody wanted to enter. In the morning the experience was repeated.

On the third night, by permission of the priest, I performed the ceremonies unaided. I decked the bed of the Lord with garlands till everything looked beautiful. I was sure the Lord would be pleased with this service. The room was locked, and the priest took away the key. I squatted on the floor as usual, and the same signs heralded His coming. The door opened at His knock. I stood aghast while it was silently closed; then I heard the creaking noise of the bed as if someone was lying down on it. I moved to the door and could hear sounds quite clearly as though someone was turning over from side to side. The whole atmosphere was surcharged with perfume. I watched with rapt attention. There was no doubt in my mind that the Lord was enjoying His rest. In the morning the door opened and was shut again; the sound of the Lord's pattens was heard going away, and sweet perfume filled the air. The Lord had gone.

The priest came with his lantern as usual. We had our bath, then entered the holy bedroom. As soon as the door was unlocked, the priest was taken aback with surprise. There lay the pillows as if they had been used; the bed-sheet was crushed, and the shawl looked as if someone had worn it and thrown it away in a hurry. The priest congratulated me on my devotion. He told me that he had never before witnessed such a beautiful realisation. I told him everything that had happened, and tears came to his eyes while he listened to my story.

The next day, an offer came from a Mahatma who was abbot of a very rich monastery in the neighbourhood. He wanted to make me his chief disciple, which meant an income of £ 2000 a year. Usually a revelation is followed by an equivalent temptation to test the initiate, and make sure that pride has not resulted instead of humility from the divine favour; just as after the acceptance of my service on Mount Girnar came the offer of the post of Extra Assis-

The God's Bed

tant Commissioner, so now came this offer of the second position in this wealthy foundation.

I sent a humble refusal and took leave of my friend the old priest, and with his blessing departed.

15

Mysticism is not Mystery, it is Mystery Unveiled

I DESIRED and received—this was neither fantasy nor hallucination, but reality. If I cannot believe my eyes, my nose, my ears, my senses, what am I to believe? Am I to believe those wiseacres who believe things they merely think are true, and throw experience to the winds? I was not a booby to be carried off my feet by the opinions of others. Convictions had been forced on me, and I could safely depend upon them.

I had wanted to surprise the Lord sleeping, had succeeded, and apprehended thereby that He was wide-awake. I grasped His reality but at the same time knew that He was too great for my arms to embrace. And this was a considerable step towards spiritual life, and gave a violent shock to the last remaining traces of rationalism that lurked in my brain, and made room for more practical faith.

"Faith begets wisdom," so says the *Geeta*. With so many facts before me, I should have been the silliest dolt on earth had I not grasped the fundamentals of faith and tried to translate them into action. There was enough material for me to build on, and I wanted to rear the superstructure of my spiritual life on the firm foundation of faith. The conflict between doubt and faith was getting every day more serious, and my doubts as actual experiences consolidated began slowly to give way. Light dawned upon me. The shadows of materialism faded away, and along with it the ignorance that it brought in its train; my intellect was purified and began to merge itself in faith. "Have faith, have faith! and thou shalt see Him!" cried my friend and guide, and those blessed words always rang in my ears. Besides, a host of rishis, saints and mahatmas had all said the same things.

On my return through the forest, I stumbled accidentally on a Mahatma. He was naked. His eyes looked feverish; perhaps he was looking at something which did not belong to this world. He clapped his hands when he saw me. I went near and offered my salutations. He whispered: "Oh, there is a child coming, one of God's beloved is fighting," as if to himself, but I knew they were intended for me. He knew me, gave me his message, then hurried away. I looked after him in amazement, but he was already out of sight. How had he disappeared in so short a time? Here was another corroboration. To believe or not to believe, was the question. I decided to believe, notwithstanding the world.

I came to Darwha and wanted to pay my respects to a Mahatma there. I stayed with a friend of mine who was a practising pleader. He welcomed me, and when I told him whom I wished to see, he sent his clerk to find out if the Mahatma was in the tavern, for he passed most of his time there. People offered him drink which he accepted with relish, but it had no effect on his reason, nor did he need to discharge the liquid. He had been watched for hours after imbibing a huge quantity and not been seen to relieve himself. This is not recounted of Socrates, whose mind was reputed equally immune from the fumes of alcohol. This Mahatma's wisdom was held in reverence by rich and poor alike, yet his favourite resort was the taverns and his chosen disciples drunkards. To sober men he said: "You are virtuous, you need no wisdom; but these offer me the best they have, which is liquor, and I give them my best in return, which is spiritual life."

The news came that the Mahatma was not there. Messengers were sent all over the town, but there was no trace of him. I refused to take my milk before I had offered it first to him.

Evening came and my host was trying to persuade me to break my fast, though I still refused, when we heard hurried steps on the staircase. The Mahatma, Shri Lalamaharaj, entered, dressed in dirty rags, his breath emitting a strong smell of liquor. I fell at his feet and told him how grateful I was for his gracious visit. He smiled and asked me to drink my milk first, as I was hungry. I offered it to him first, then drank it after he had tasted it.

He used words but not sentences, so that the sense could only be followed by those who had a concentrated sympathy with the speaker. Once he had aroused such sympathy it was possible to follow his thought a long while, though he omitted all but the principal words. This method is used by many Mahatmas, as it enables them to converse intimately with one though many are present. He knew where the struggle in my mind raged most fiercely, and asked me to marry and lead a house-holder's life. He gave me his assurance that it would not hinder my spiritual life, and that my Divine Master could rescue me out of all temptations. He asked my friend the pleader to bring him scented oil and turmeric, and besmeared my arm with it as they do in marriage ceremonies. I thought in spite of my efforts my fate was drawing me to married life, and there was no remedy but to submit.

The Mahatma talked for a couple of hours, gave me a few hints about meditation, and with a blessing departed. How marvellously he had come and delivered his message. I remember he said to me that real mysticism was not mystery, but mystery unveiled, and once a mystery is unveiled it no longer remains a mystery but is plain and simple knowledge. I thought within myself, that it was the fault of the learned that they made so great a mystery out of very plain matters. They wrote volume after volume about the fact which the Vedas have proclaimed to the world in three words: "Thou Art That",[1] which in its context means "O Man, thou art Brahma, the Divine Spirit." When people are afraid of facing a fact directly, they try to create a halo of mysticism about it, and thus hide their ignorance from the public. I had started out to realise God. There were ups and downs, desires and ambitions, but I was determined to face all the risks, and marriage was one of the great risks that I faced.

My mind was still struggling between religion and spirituality. So I came to Amraoti. My parents welcomed me back and were glad to hear what I had seen, but in their heart of hearts they felt sure that I was to leave them. My mother did not take any food, nor even water, for some days, and when I was told of this it quite unnerved me. I thought I was the cause of bringing so much misery to those who loved me so dearly and sacrificed everything for my comfort. Marriage was a religious duty which I owed to them.

---

[1] That is, *Tat Ivam Asi. Editor.*

I went to my mother with tears in my eyes and apologised for my faults, and asked her if I could do anything for her. She took a promise from me that I would obey her, and then asked me to marry for her sake. I told her that it seemed to me too late, since I had succeeded in controlling myself and did not feel the necessity of entering into the bonds of matrimony. This made her the more miserable, and, though loath to do so, I had to keep my promise and obey the Mahatma of Darwha. Shortly after I was marred in Poona.

A new chapter in life began, and I was determined to write it as finely as I could, and felt sure that my Divine Master was bound to save me in the end.

7. Parvati (Godavari) Purohit in middle age.

16

Religion versus Spirituality

MY father took a two years' furlough, and we all went to live at Poona. The eldest of our family clan was my grandmother's maternal uncle Annasahib Bhatavdekar, at that time eighty years of age, who lived there, and with whom I had often stayed and was a favourite. In compliment to this old gentleman's venerable sagacity, my parents asked him to choose me a wife from among the many suitable matches which had been canvassed when my relatives had first expected me to marry, all of whom at that time I had refused to consider. But now my mind had changed, and his choice fell on Godu Bai, a girl of sixteen, of well-to-do family. Her father was so surprised, having understood that I was a convinced celibate, that he came to make sure that there was no mistake; and I was able to satisfy him both of my good faith and of the constancy of my desire for a spiritual life. Godu was of a cheery disposition, perfectly healthy, a great favourite among her school friends, clever with the needle, expert in the kitchen, and was in every way a good match except that she had no dowry; but that was a consideration that did not weigh with me.

At our first meeting I gave her my promise before the sacred fire, the Brahmins and God. Thenceforward, in spite of the urge of renunciation that swelled in my breast, I was in duty bound to keep it. I loved her dearly, though determined that our love should never come under the sway of engrossing physical passion. I tried to coach her in my ideals, and being a lady bred in Hindu culture, she earnestly tried to assimilate them. She became a member of our household, the companion of my four sisters. All relationships should, as we think, be governed by a voluntary order, which is not enforced but accepted gladly with a view to prevent affection becoming selfish and exclusive. The mother-in-law yields up her keys and authority to her son's wife, who in turn would not think of acting without having consulted her husband's mother. My father in the same way put all the household business in my hands, and I consulted and deferred to his wishes. A young couple never speak to one another before their elders, though they can communicate by glance and demeanour; for we Hindus read each other's faces far better and more easily than the European would seem to.

I and my wife had little of one another's company till we had locked up at night, and if I went to my room very late and my wife was already asleep in my sister's room my mother would rise and go there and wake her and bring her to my room. All these customs had been evolved to prevent affection becoming exclusive or disruptive of the general peace of the household. When two married brothers live in the father's house, the children of the elder will be taught always to ask their uncle, the younger, to satisfy their material wants; to him they go for toys and sweets, etc., and vice versa, so that they may love their parents, yet run no risk of being spoiled by them, and also have good reason to love and look up to their uncles. Thus less partiality is shown in the expression of affection, and general goodwill reigns.

The household at Poona consisted of my parents, myself and wife, my four sisters who, though married, came frequently either with their husbands or without, and my youngest brother. There were besides a large number of guests always staying in the house for long or short periods. When we young people received, my mother would arrange to visit a friend so that we might make as much noise as we liked, and when my friends came to visit me, my father would remain in his rooms on the top floor. Thus respect became a pleasure and it was returned, and goodwill and cheerfulness flourished.

Not only did the business of the house absorb much of my time, but I now had other business to attend to. Though my father had refused the Extra Assistant Commissionership with which I had been tempted after Mount Girnar, though after the revelation at Mahur I had refused the abbot of the monastery's offer, and in spite of having clearly perceived the futility of mantrams as aids to spiritual results, I now wavered and took to repeating a mantram which controlled worldly prosperity. Immediately a friend of my father's arrived and offered me a partnership in a business he had formed to exploit a railway contract; he hoped thus to repay my father who, when he was in danger of going to gaol, had stood between him and his deserts and so, during the first part of our stay in Poona, I had to busy myself with calculations and bookkeeping and received sufficient money. I gave over repeating that mantram, and immediately my father's friend faced about and put me out of his business, treating me with no little injustice and confirming me in my faith that the use of mantrams was of small value in obtaining spiritual results.

No money, no life, is the order of this world. When I told my wife that I did not intend to earn money and that I would rather lead the life of a recluse, she was surprised, but tried to assimilate my spirit. Money was the tap-root of all misery, said the Mahatmas. And passion for woman the next longest. I was convinced of the efficacy of strict continence, and knew it helped concentration. Mind as distinct from spirit is a fine form of matter. The sages say it is the direct product of semen. Sexual intercourse meant so much expenditure of vital energy, which, though it is refunded, soon loses its primal excellence; we see that primal excellence in many Mahatmas, who retain the qualities of youth up to a hundred years of age and beyond. Though still a novice, I could very well understand that the more you wanted to concentrate all the forces of your mind, the greater the necessity of conserving your energy, that Brahmacharya, or strict celibacy, was the only way to real spiritual progress.

The religious code of married life dragged me the other way. No householder is allowed to renounce unless with the permission of his wife and after he has first begotten a son. Celibacy has a high spiritual significance, but marriage was instituted for the preservation of the race. And I thought that if I was not able to convince a soul so near and dear to me, about the righteousness of my ambition, it would be nonsense to pretend to do good to the world at large.

Thus the conflict continued for six months. I was absolutely honest with my wife. We talked during that period throughout whole nights on end, at the same time observing the strictest celibacy, and when I found that she responded finely to what I said, I thought it time to enter on the life of a householder, which was to be renounced with the consent of my wife after a son had been begotten.

There were three irons in my fire: public service, family service and service of God. I was still bound down to this earth. Was not the service of mankind the service of God? I seriously pondered over this idea and met those who believed in philanthropy and asked them whether they had seen God, and they dared not say that they had. Everybody answered my question in his own way, but no one convinced me. I asked them if they had attained peace, and nobody could say that he had. There was no peace, no bliss, in spite of their efforts to help mankind. Either they did not wholly know what they aimed at, or were the dupes of empty speculations. Though they never attained the goal, had they gone too far to retrace their footsteps? I could very well picture their position. I thought there must be something often in such a philosophy, or else in the way they worked it out, and was not satisfied with their results.

The great principles of Hindu philosophy came to my rescue. Everybody said that God is omniscient, omnipresent and omnipotent; and granting all these attributes, how is it that man was trying to help Him amend this world of His? Is He not powerful enough Himself? I came to the conclusion that it was sheer ignorance and egoism when men talked about helping Him or helping mankind. When you begin to do good to this world, you presuppose that you are sufficiently wise to understand it, and powerful enough to help it out of its difficulties. Such men profess too much.

The world is full of misery. What is the reason? Perhaps those people who want to help are the cause, and, when bad results of their actions appear, they resort to the same despotic benevolence as a remedy. Thus misery is piled on misery, all the product of ignorance and egoism, as the sages said, and as I felt forced to agree.

I had to chalk out my own line. I thought, yes, the world has been created by Him, and He alone is able to help it. Then what business have I to meddle unless He bids me? My first duty is to know Him, and attain direct communication with Him. In short, I thought I should have His *adesha*, or mandate, before I did anything for this world. I had already had some glimpses of Him, and I thought I ought to build up permanent relations with Him; these alone might conduce not only to my individual welfare, but to the welfare of my nearest and dearest and the whole world.

Then the second problem came before me, and I solved it according not to my opinion but that of my religious preceptors. I knew that I should have to retrace my steps, but there was no remedy. Indulgence in sensual pleasure adds to the appetite for it, and all your honesty of purpose and sense of duty has not the power to check the expenditure of your mental and physical energies in the pleasure of a moment. But the time was not yet, and I had to wait.

My parents were very glad that my marriage bound me to my home with golden chains. They had forged those chains, and only through filial duty had they been able to enthrall me with them. They knew that I still clung to my ideal, and was trying hard to realise it. They had full faith in my strength of purpose and knew that I would rather die in the attempt than give it up. At the same time my heart knew that my difficulties would be added to by the indulgence of my senses. But He knew all, and I had firm faith in Him.

17

The Kundalini

I HAD to realise the Divine Master through my material senses, yet He transcended all matter. A line is length without breadth, but when you want to prove a proposition you have to endow it with breadth, otherwise no demonstration is possible. By analogy we endow God with a name and a form to meditate on Him, with the help of eyes, ears and tongue. I needed to gaze on His form steadily, hear His word frequently, repeat His name incessantly, and thus approach His presence.

I repeated the Gayatri, the most sacred mantram, and became so habituated that even in my dreams I continued. When talking with others, my mind went on unconsciously muttering: "We meditate on the Supreme splendour of that divine Being; may it illuminate our intellects." Every day brought a new charm. The taste of my tongue was refined. I found even the sweet things that I had been too fond of were no longer sweet; but food or no food, in my mouth I often relished savours which ravished the sense. This material body is composed of five principle elements—earth, water, light, air and *akasha*. The virtue of earth is fragrance; of water, fineness of taste; of light, beauty; of air, touch; and of *akasha*, music. Slowly but surely the five elements began to refine in me till I enjoyed the sweet odours of several flowers when none were present. The more I concentrated my attention on the Lord, the more beautiful were the forms I beheld floating in the light, so much so that those who pass for beautiful upon this earth appeared ugly by contrast. In time my whole body was so thrilled with a sense of contacts that the embraces of my wife had no charm for me. And the invisible musicians so played as to convince me that our Indian instruments must have been invented by those who in former ages heard the music I now listened to: the *veena*, the conch, the humming of the bee, the sound of ocean waves, and the drum concerted together to enchant me, where no one was playing, and though they performed hour after hour, there was nothing to pay.

In this way my senses were weaned from gross pleasures. I could enjoy more excellent ones without cost and without exhaustion. I had been wont to wonder how the ascetics endured complete solitude. How were their senses satisfied? From the first it had seemed probable that they were enjoying higher pleasures than those of ordinary men; but now the reality was revealed to me, and my contentment knew no bounds. Still I feared that my married life was delaying my spiritual progress. Thank Heaven, the flame of spirituality had been kept always burning in my heart. I was practising the yogi postures, and I would settle into Siddhasana, or the great posture of the Adepts or Mahatmas, with immense satisfaction. From the seat the torso is erect, the feet with their soles turned upward rest in a valley formed between thigh and calf; the arms either folded across the chest or with the wrists resting below the knee letting the hands drop naturally. Though it may suggest the appearance, this description is so rough that no one by its aid could reproduce the posture, which may have dangerous results if not correctly assumed.

I had renounced solid food already and was taking milk only, with fruit occasionally. My body grew more and more delicate, so much so that I could no longer digest an apple but vomited. Buffalo's milk disagreed with me; cow's milk suited me better. I had no inclination to speak or stir about. Such pleasures were stored within me that this beggarly world had nothing superior to offer. This was the natural order of renunciation. There was no virtue in it; worldly pleasures were renounced because finer were enjoyed.

Some praised me, others censured. I subtracted the latter from the former, and the result was nil. Ignorance was only to be pitied and not found fault with. There was no need to listen to a world I had renounced. This renouncement was not due to hatred for the world, but because it had proved too poor to attract me. The world had been willing to love me, but I had started in search of a higher love which, when found, confirmed me in the way I had taken.

My inner life was developing fast. I wept and wept. I could not longer bear the pangs of separation from the Divine Master, and slept very little. The flesh was an agony; the senses, coals of fire; with bones shattered to pieces, blood boiling, and tears that never ceased, my whole frame received electric shocks difficult to sustain. I refused to speak. My legs refused to carry my weight; hunger became a torment; the fire of the mystic Kundalini, the serpentine fire, was mounting within me.

I underwent pangs as of death every moment, weeping and praying, praying and weeping ceaselessly. My beloved friend arrived from Sangli in southern Maharatta all of a sudden after so many months. He had already attained the goal of his life. He and his Master were one. I ran to him and embraced him frantically. He placed his palm on my head, and in a gentle and musical voice asked me: "Do you believe now that your Divine Master loves you?" I looked at him with the utmost affection, and he was satisfied with the answer.

The aged Rao Rambha Nimbalker of Hyderabad sent an offer to me. Our family had relations with his house. He wanted me to stay at Poona and was willing to defray expenses, and to give me 500 rupees per month as pocket-money if I would take charge of his legal affairs. I sent him a refusal, though I feared it would pain him. His Exalted Highness, the late Nizam, sent a messenger to desire me to go to Hyderabad, and was willing to give a jagir, and enable me to live right royally like my grandfather. I thanked him but refused. He sent a second messenger, promising anything in his power; I remained firm and, thanking him, replied: "God is able to give me all that I desire."

18

Truth knows no Defence

For nearly three months I had to undergo these severe pangs. Rude shocks were breaking up the habits that my mind had formed in childhood, and the ingrained character of its motion was being purified. My body felt no inclination to activity or to any thought. In fact, the senses refused to function.

Slowly I began to recover and to see things in their reality. Without effort on my part, quite naturally, I recommenced to meditate as before. In the meantime, my wife had gone to her parents and she came back with a sweet little daughter. Dear Indumati was a darling, very cheerful, and looked beautiful with a pearl necklace round her neck which my father had given her. A child was in the house and meant an accession of comfort for my parents. What is a home without a child? As they say: "The mother is glorified by the child, the child by the mother's nearness, and both together transfigure the home."

My mind ceased to wander from place to place. That centre, whence so many desires had surged, fell quiet; thither peace had come and soon was everywhere. Peace reigned in the household because I no longer made demands on anybody. In the world there was peace because I never desired to meddle there; within my soul also, because that is the proper home of peace; surely I was fast approaching the original source from which all serenity flows! So many years had gone in ransacking the world where only cruel wrongs were discovered, but at length peace was almost clasped far within, where is neither change of place nor of season.

Anchored to meditation, the name of the Lord never left my lips. His form was always before me; His presence guarded me on all sides and was my sustenance. No more oscillations, no more arguments, no more hypotheses, but real experience, like that we all have of common things and daily events.

Months flowed into months. I never noted when sun rose or when it set. Taking half a pound of milk and a few nimb leaves a day, I sat absorbed in meditation as my wife did in the next room, her diet the same as mine. We got up punctually at 3 A.M. and, after our bath, began to meditate at 4 A.M. At 10.30 we breakfasted on four ounces of milk, took a second bath at noon, and meditated till 4.30 P.M. Then came a second meal of four ounces of milk, and a third bath in the evening at six o'clock, with meditation till 10 P.M. Dinner followed of the remaining eight ounces of milk. Comfortably we each lay down on separate beds in neighbouring rooms on Persian carpets, over which were spread tigers' skins, and these in turn were covered with pure white bedsheets. We had two soft pillows a-piece. At times I read the yoga-aphorisms of Patanjali till 11 P.M., which was the time when I usually went to sleep. We used to lock the front door of the house so that nobody should disturb us. And what on earth could they disturb us for?

I was a householder, and as such if any guest came he was bound to have a welcome. One day a friend of mine came. He was welcomed by my wife. We offered him half of our milk. He could only withstand the pressure of his hunger till evening, then he hurried away in silence. I told him that I had nothing more to offer, because I was poor. I was not supposed to beg, borrow or steal; but still I was willing to do my duty towards him.

Another gentleman came, with the news that he had realised God. I gave him the honour that was his due, but he was not satisfied. He wanted to exploit my name as his disciple. There he was disappointed. Then he started to revile me, writing innumerable letters to my friends and relatives, accusing me of taking money from my disciples, though I had none. One of the newspapers printed one of his letters. Some of my friends threatened to prosecute the editor. He came to me and apologised. I told him that I was dead civilly. "So long as you write about me, you are safe, but do no make the same experiment upon others, in that case the prison doors are likely to open for you. Neither your praise nor your censure can affect me, for I do not believe in either." He had come to me in fear, but we parted friends.

Truth knows no Defence

My father had returned to Amraoti. Some men went to him and reviled me. He calmly answered them: "I know my son better." I tried to deserve his faith in me and repeated to myself: "Truth needs no defence." Though he sorrowed because his worldly ambitions were thwarted by my conduct, yet he knew that I was not pursuing any wrong path, and in his heart of hearts approved.

One day I went out to take the air. I had not stirred out for months. In the streets I met friends and acquaintances who saluted me; I returned their salutations, but my memory failed to recognise them. My friend was with me and wondered that I asked him who they were. But when I failed to recognise my brother-in-law and asked him what his name was, I grew afraid of this state of oblivion and felt I had not kept a proper balance, and thenceforth decided to walk abroad more frequently. Though disinclined to talk, I now conversed a little with my friends in the evening, though only about the spiritual life. To leave a secluded life and reaccommodate myself to the old environment was a slow process. I avoided all controversial subjects; for my mind was purged of all the past associations and must be kept free from uncongenial thoughts, as my mission in life was wholly spiritual. My beloved friend, guide and philosopher came to help me, and I soon found that there was no question he could not answer, no difficulty he failed to solve.

19

My Master

THERE were many roads to spiritual life mapped out in the various books, but I was in search of someone who had actually reached the goal and returned and who had had similar needs to my own. I had already requested many Mahatmas to accept me as disciple, but they had said that I belonged to another. Thereupon I had in my under-graduate days accepted Lord Dattatreya as my guru and my guide. But this involved praying for days together before any direction reached me in a vision, and these injunctions consisted of a single word or at most two. The utmost good sense was required in interpreting them, and left me afraid lest I might have misunderstood them. But now my Divine Master appeared to me in a vision and told me that He had handed me over to the care of my friend, and that as He had already blessed him there was no difference between them, they were now as one. I told my friend this; he merely smiled, and releasing myself from his embrace, I knelt down before him as his disciple.

My master had been born of a very rich and pious family. His father was a pleader with a large practice, and was the head of a family noted for its righteousness, hospitality and charity. He had one elder brother and seven sisters, but he was the best-beloved of his parents. He lived from his earliest youth under a very strict discipline, and was always happy and joyous. After the death of his father, he signed a blank paper and handed it to his elder brother, and whatever share the latter was pleased to allow him was cheerfully accepted. Thus the partition was effected. The two brothers differed diametrically from each other, so far as their outlook on life was concerned.

My master was already married and was leading a well-to-do life to all outward appearances. He had two daughters and a son, and I know his wife loved and adored him. But his soul was craving for something higher. Gradually the light dawned upon him and, after failing in his matriculation examination, he left the University and went out to achieve spirituality. Before long he felt the urge so strongly that he decided to give up all worldly life and strive for realisation. He then gave his property in charity and, keeping only enough to maintain himself, his wife and children above want, he began to meditate on Lord Dattatreya, whom he took as his *gurudeo* or Divine Master. His wife, too, was highly spiritual and tried to help her husband and lord in his spiritual aspirations. She led a very strict life and renounced all worldly ambitions in the pursuit of a higher and purer life.

Her husband associated himself with some of the most famous Mahatmas and took the primary lessons in yoga from them. When I first met him, as a result of a long course of strict austerity and concentration, he was already initiated, and in direct touch with the Divine Master.

My master had travelled throughout the length and breadth of the country with his begging-bowl, and visited nearly all the places of pilgrimage. He thus encountered experience after experience and learned to translate the great principles into practical life. He talked very little and acted what he preached. Always cheerful and at peace in his mind under even the hardest trials, he was sincere, pure, straightforward and full of devotion towards his Divine Master; he secured realisation and was ever ready to die rather than yield to the debilitating influences of the world.

At Poona my master was staying at our house. One day he suddenly said: "I must set out to Junnar", and he ordered a carriage and left us without further explanation. I afterwards learned from another Mahatma's disciple that his master had on that day been waiting by the roadside at Junnar for a week expecting that my master would come along the road from Poona; my informant had wondered why his master should wait by the roadside day after day. When my master's carriage came this Mahatma rose up, my master got down; they gazed at each other and satisfied one another's minds without words. What higher means of communication they used he did not know. Mahatmas often do not tell their disciples and hearers that another master is present. Once at Shirdi, in a deserted mosque, a Mahatma with a very great following was teaching. He suddenly said: "My father is here!"—"Have you got a father?"—"He is both mine and the father of all."—"Where is he?"—"Here and everywhere."—"What is his trade?"—"He tends a flock."—"He is keeping sheep."—"Why not—he tends the whole world." Then my master caught his eye and he fell silent, for he knew that he was not to reveal then and there of whom he had spoken.

On another occasion I was travelling with my master at Amraoti. He went to the temple every day where a seat was prepared for him, and after the sermon on *Geeta* was over he sat still while all the people came to touch his feet. But one day he became restless during the service and whispered to me: "I must go...I am needed," and at the end he got up and pushed through the crowd, I following him and all the people after us. He walked so fast that I could hardly keep up with him, and though the big boys ran in order to keep alongside they were all left behind. Presently he stopped, turned aside under some trees, and closed his eyes; then after a minute or two said to me: "All is over." I wondered, but a little later heard the mourning from a house near by where a disciple of his had been lying sick unto death. He had come there, as I now understood, to help that disciple's soul to leave his body, for he said: "Ah, what a brave soul!" This man, as I afterwards learned, had in his last minutes forgotten wife, brother and children in order to fix his mind on my master, who therefore had felt impelled to hasten to his aid in that last struggle with death.

We were at Satara. Here I found Joshi, a disciple of my master, who though a graduate, held a post-office clerkship at a very low salary and was dying of consumption. He could not afford a nurse, and I went to live with him so as to render him the services he needed. He was very ill and suffered terribly. After three months I wrote to our master and told him that the case was desperate; he came immediately and told Joshi: "I will lie down on your bed and bear these sufferings instead of you, if you can no longer bear them; you can have health and relief." But Joshi replied: "No, they are my Karma and I will not inflict them on him whom I love best." For a week yet he endured his agony, then our master returned one night and found him very restless, and said: "Are you willing to go?"

"Yes", the sufferer replied, "whenever it pleases you."—"Well, then, tomorrow at sunrise." That would be on Thursday, therefore, sacred to Lord Dattatreya, but in this case "Ekadashi", that is, sacred to Lord Shrikrishna also. The night was very restless, and he asked me to sing the hymns. At last, at 5.30, he begged me to go and fetch our master, who came at once and spoke to him for about half an hour about the love of God, then placed his hand on his breast just as the sun peeped over the horizon, and the spirit gently slipped from the body.

My master passed every coin we received to me to keep, but it produced a burning in my flesh at whatever point was nearest to where I had placed it. It is also recorded of Shri Ramakrishna Paramahamsa that he felt a great revulsion from any seat on which a bad man had been seated, and that his fingers twisted and contorted on contact with coins, and that he completely overcame these revulsions, the last shadow left by the austerities that had freed him from the fear of evil. So now in my own humble way I had to overcome the ache that a coin produced by its proximity, the lingering reaction left by those great struggles I had undergone to overcome my natural inclination to love wealth and good living. But my master was at my side, and so the victory was assured.

To give up the position of a friend which meant equality of status, and surrender myself to him as a servant, pained me a little in the beginning, but I felt compelled in view of the wide gulf which separated me from one who had realised our Lord. So I threw aside the manners of friendship and assumed those of discipleship. For was it not a form of egoism to remain on equal terms where no equality existed? Then why not face facts and admit that I was a mere disciple.

20

Samadhi

My master continued to treat me as a friend though I treated him as a disciple should; in fact, he never exercised the authority of a master. Whenever he came to our house, I gave up my meditation to wait upon him. We talked for days and nights together about his experiences on his travels. He commanded my rapt attention, since I hoped to follow in his steps on the same roads. Whenever he spoke about our Divine Master, tears came to his eyes, his hair stood on end and his whole frame shook with emotion, and many a time he passed into *samadhi*, the highest stage of spiritual ecstasy. I gazed on him unceasingly and thought I could have contemplated him forever, so renewing was the perfect peace on his face. His body was like a marble statue and his breath emitted the sweetest perfumes and enchanted me. I used to burn the musk incense of which he was so fond, and the whole atmosphere became rapturously spiritual. His features would become so brilliant that all the divinity in the world seemed to radiate from them. An insignificant creature kneeling before the Lord, I worshipped him; for had not the Lord Himself told me that He had blessed him, and that there was no difference between them?

Often when I prepared a bath for him, he went into *samadhi*, and I repeated the sacred Vedas and the hymns in praise of him, and when I had finished he slowly returned to this world. He compared himself to an instrument played on by the Divine Hand, disclaiming all individuality of his own since he had dedicated himself mind and body and soul to his Divine Master.

Once he was sitting in Siddhasana posture and passed into *samadhi*. Accidentally I touched one of his hands, and it fell from his lap as if it was dislocated and dead. After he came out of his *samadhi*,

Samadhi

I had to massage it before it recovered. Thenceforward I was very much afraid of him when in *samadhi*, and did not dare to touch him.

On another occasion his head was lying on my lap and we were talking about the life of Lord Dattatreya. He knew many anecdotes of the Divine Life, and I was listening with rapt attention, when all of a sudden he slipped into *samadhi*. I knew that if I stirred it would mean havoc to his head. I dared not move a hair's breadth. I was gazing at his beautiful face which was shining. One hour passed away in that state, then another. I was not strong enough to support his head for such a long time, but there was no alternative. My thighs ached, but I strengthened myself to endure through the hours of trial. At last I watched his beautiful eyes opening with delight and relief. He embraced me, and threw such a loving glance at me that all the pain I had undergone vanished in a moment.

He at times spoke on the philosophy of devotion, and gave examples from the lives of devotees, such as Shri Shukacharya who was very proud that his father, Shri Vyasa, the author of *Mahabharata*, was his guru, and before he was sixteen had made astonishing progress in the spiritual life. Vyasa then said to him: "I have taught you all I can; if anything is needed to perfect you, King Janaka can instruct you in it." Shukacharya wondered that a king could teach him more than a saint like his father, but determined to walk to the court, and when he found his father following him, deeply lamenting the separation from his son, he wondered how it was that his father behaved like an ordinary man as though he were still attached to material presences. The road led him by a river where women were bathing. Though they saw him naked as themselves, they took no notice; yet as soon as his father approached, they hurried on their clothes though he was an old white-haired man. Shukacharya could not help wondering. Presently his father returned home from following him. In time he arrived at the court and sent in a message, but the Rajah took no notice but left him standing at the gate. At this he wondered and ere long passed into *samadhi*. After three days he was sent for and received with all honour; then when he was stretched upon a couch, the Rajah's queen approached to shampoo his feet. She, seeing him so young and beautiful, felt as his mother might and would have embraced him, but he turned his back on her. Immediately Lord Dattatreya was manifested, and said: "How you scorn the mother's love?" And behold, his father also suddenly appeared in the room. Then Shukacharya understood that on each occasion when he wondered he had proved that his mind was not spiritually free, but was still held by an habitual reaction instead of accepting the fact as a fact, that in refusing the mother's embrace his puritanical reaction had caused him to act unkindly. Thus did he receive, in the court of King Janaka, the lesson needed to free his spirit from the habitual reactions which had been lodged in him by the austere discipline to which his father had submitted him, and by which he had attained to all but perfect holiness.

On other occasions he expounded the yogic aphorisms of Patanjali, or elucidated the fundamental principle "Thou art That", by which we realise the divine destiny and immediate duties of human life. Before all else he laid stress on practice and urged me to realise rather than to discuss. For the world is always only too inclined to appreciate crude and abstract philosophy rather than to translate precept into word and deed.

The company of my master was a constant pleasure. Every little problem is important, and to solve each by oneself requires great expenditure of time, energy and intellect. But he was ready to make the way easy for me. In their eagerness to realise, students of yoga imagine that they have attained a higher stage than in fact is the case, and need to be brought down time after time to the bottom of the ladder; hence the necessity of a guru. A guide is needed in order to attain proficiency in science; then why should we shrink back from choosing one for our spiritual studies. A guru is not a tyrant, neither is a disciple a slave. The master is also friend and guide, and the disciple is loved. If the disciple wants of his own accord to take up a humbler position, it is not the fault of the guru. The relation is voluntary; though there be no limit to the reverence that a disciple can give, there is none to the liberty that the master may allow. The psychological adjustment meets each particular case, and onlookers have rarely any ground to find fault.

My master had determined on a journey through Maharashtra, and to travel in his company had long seemed to me the height of bliss. But I could not leave my meditation unless and until he wished me to do so. At last I had his leave. In fact, the strictness of

Samadhi

my seclusion for meditation had almost incapacitated me for life abroad. I needed a change and exercise, and in no other form could it so exactly have answered my needs both physical and spiritual.

21

The Touchstone

TRAVEL was a great change, too great a change, for I was physically unfit for walking and felt no inclination for exercise, but soon I rediscovered my muscles. I had nothing to complain of; in fact, all was a pleasure for me. Though we met many who talked about spirituality, to be obliged to listen only added strength to my resolves. The funniest thing was when people came to learn and remained to preach. The great sages of old were very wise in not preaching to everybody. Even in universities nobody is allowed to enjoy the privilege of the higher stages unless he has gone through the preliminary course. But many are wonderstruck when they learn that the same holds good for students in the knowledge of God.

A great spiritual wave was passing through the minds of Indians at that time. Everybody was on the look-out for the next *avatar*, or incarnation of God, who they thought must descend to this earth in order to bless it. Every Mahatma talked of this, which was their panacea for all evils. All sane people thought that He must incarnate Himself and put new life into the Indians and re-establish the great eternal truths of religion. And they were right. Lord Shrikrishna has given them a promise in the *Geeta* to that effect. Indians have always believed that great promise and have anxiously waited for the new era of divine life; for had not India always been saved by spirituality? But where to find the new *avatar* perplexed them all. Only the great sages understood, but they kept silence. The way to understand a Mahatma is to serve him and love, and to draw him out in privacy. He will never reveal himself until the psychological moment arrives, and there is no power on earth which can force him against his will. I was so sure of this that I took the safe way and found out the secret, kept it, and repeated in the recesses of my heart, "Not yet."

Most beautiful were my master's encounters with various saints. I do not presume to say that I understood everything that passed between them, but I gleaned a little. Some of the saints were so eager to have a sight of my master that they would wait on the road for days, telling nobody why they did so, and keeping even their disciples in ignorance. After the meeting was over, these disciples would try to have their say, but were little understood even among themselves. Their hearts overflowed, and in failing they were learning how to control them.

The saints conversed on the spiritual plane, which was a sealed book to me. We all believe in speech by word of mouth and do not even dream of higher forms of communication. Those who are versed in these, use the lower ones very sparingly. Many people came to my master with their questions, but all were easily answered. He pleaded his ignorance about books, but his talk corroborated the wisdom they contain. His experience was the source from which he drew, and such knowledge is first-hand. He stated facts and never deduced theories.

All the wisdom of the Vedas, the Upanishads and the *Geeta* flowed around me while with my master, for he was full of them and in harmony with their spirit. I felt proud that the rare privilege of serving such a master had been mine. When the strictness of discipleship wearied me, I could retreat into familiarity with my friend, for he was ready to adjust himself to my needs. So simple, so adequate, so majestic, and to crown all so humble, that though our bodies were two, they seemed to be swayed by one soul. His spirit worked unostentatiously but the results astounded me.

My master, when he was in the mood, told me certain things. These glimpses into the unseen made me happy and refreshed my zest in studying the alphabet of the universal mystery. Every revelation was solely due to the grace of my master. How can the debt I owe him ever be paid? Since this is impossible, I no longer desire to free myself from it, for we must accept our limitations.

I had not travelled for years, and now was incessantly on the move, partaking of whatever food might be available: a severe trial for my delicate digestion. There was discussion everywhere; I had to put up with that too though so desiring peaceful meditation. The presence and service of my master redeemed and compensated for all I had to undergo. Mahatma understands Mahatma, and I had the privilege of being present at such meetings, and they greatly enhanced my faith in and love for my master. All glory to him!

22

For My Sake

AFTER six months' travel, my master bade me return home, and so with a heavy heart I parted from him. My zest for wandering had vanished, and I never felt again the lure it had exerted over me in earlier days. I longed for solitude. This world was too big and heavy for me. I yearned to be alone with my God; prolonged separation from Him was unbearable.

Once more I shrank from stirring out into the streets. My happiness was within me, yet still I feared to become unbalanced; the only remedy was to seek the air and sun, and to try still to harbour the divine while mixing with my fellows. That this would be difficult I knew, but also that it was not impossible. The most difficult path has always tempted my ambition to prove my strength. Experimenting little by little, I ultimately triumphed. In meditation, worldly thoughts were not allowed to approach, and I would not allow the divine consciousness to forsake me when abroad; mentally repeating the name of my Lord, even while my lips were speaking to friends. The thread of my conversation was never lost through attention to the inner music. His grace enabled me to return and satisfy my interlocutor before he noticed my muteness. The borderland between the two worlds was slippery; the discipline exacted by constant perils was rigorous, but Heaven helped me.

All men are adepts in renunciation; but alas, they renounce the right path in order to follow the wrong! We find it easier to renounce the divine self than the other. The habit is then acquired by constant repetition till we mistake ignorance for wisdom, worldliness for spirituality, expediency for duty, illusion for truth and sensation for bliss; this has been going on since the dawn of history, and will end only with its end.

I was trying to swim up-stream, away from the wide water towards the source. Physical, moral and spiritual forces were latent in me as in each of us, and could only be directed by slow degrees towards their true goal. But the approach to spiritual life has peculiar dangers of its own. Visionary enjoyments cannot remain separated from manifestations of power, and the earlier occurrences of these are terrifying. My touch sufficed to accomplish things which I had never thought of doing. Some were healed, though I had not intended to help them. The saving grace in these occurrences was that I did nothing deliberately. All happened automatically. Yet the result was that I felt self-satisfied and at times elevated.

For instance, once at Bombay I was taken across the bay to watch a display of fireworks. Suddenly, before the display had begun, I felt impelled to leave the friends who had brought me there. Despite their angry protestations, I returned to the house where I was staying, to find the lady of the house alone, rolling in agony with a violent colic. She had thought of me in her distress, and at the same moment I had felt bound to return. As I bent down to lift her from the ground, she looked up at me laughingly and said: "I am so glad I thought of you; I knew you would help me, and already the terrible pain has left me." In another case, a certain man had spent much money on injections for a disease from which he suffered; they did him no good, and his doctor and his wife were in despair over his condition. The wife came to me for help. I said that I was not a doctor, but would recommend her to a friend of mine who was, and who would attend the patient without charge. My friend sent to me on seeing the patient: "You always send me to see people who are beyond medical aid." I told him to prescribe, though he was loath to do so, since our doctors neither prescribe nor charge when they consider the case hopeless. My friend wrote out the prescription at my request, and to his astonishment it had the desired effect. Similar cases occurred quite frequently.

When I weighed the utmost benefit that might possibly accrue to others from the use of these powers, against my further advance in spirituality, I felt I was being diverted from the true path. And at once I resolved to retire and go abroad no more, though new healings and miracles were demanded by those who had witnessed

For My Sake

the first or heard of them. To rescue my mind from the temptation of exerting influence for the benefit of another's body or soul, I hid myself in meditation and succeeded in preventing these new powers from running away with me.

All the sages have warned the novice not to exploit powers which he receives from practising yoga. It was now plain to me what they meant. To use spiritual power for finite ends could only distract me from pursuing relations with the infinite, I knew this power of healing was limited, and if exploited would give out, leaving me a spiritual bankrupt.

Tears and prayers should plead for me. Intense humility was the only way to complete renunciation, and must mean harshness to myself as well as to my friends. Only by refusing to deceive myself could I prevent myself deceiving others

I was staying at Lonavala, when one morning the Lord Dattatreya roused me. Great joy was mine to see Him after so long a time. I saluted. He gave me His blessing, and uttered a single word, "Write." I awoke and found Him gone.

The meaning of His command was obscure to me, for my pen had been renounced long since. Could I have heard him rightly? I thought I had not heard alright; He must know of my vow, and would never require me to break it. But the next night He appeared again, and gave the same command. There could be no mistake; but still I would not write, believing this would drive me back into the world whither I was loath to be led. All day long I argued and prayed, beseeching not to be tested too severely.

On the third night my Lord appeared and said that He had understood my reluctance, but added with a loving smile that was irresistible, "Write for my sake." I obeyed, took pencil and paper, and to my surprise began to write in English *In Quest of Myself, The Harbinger of Love* and *The Song of Silence*. Each was complete in a week. I wondered.

23

The Ordeal of Service

MY master was wont to say: "There is no novelty in spirituality, no change of programme from day to day. The more you concentrate on the Self, the more you renounce that which is not—Self. The more you meditate on God, the more you forget self-interest and the nearer is your approach to the Absolute. Firm resolution backed up by a sort of divine recklessness is the only thing needed." I found every word true.

I completed my third and fourth books of poems entitled *The Honey-Comb* and *At Thy Lotus-Feet*. Next year I wrote in Marathi, my mother tongue, many poems, a drama, a novel, a metrical translation of the *Geeta* and a commentary on it. The third year I wrote in Sanskrit, and in the fourth I wrote in Hindi, the lingua franca of India. The subject which was treated in all these books was the same: my Lord. His satisfaction with it was the only reward I looked for and all that I obtained.

Another daughter was born, a sweet child, and was named Sumati, and she was followed by the much coveted son, Chandrashekhar. He solved the great problem of my householder's life. My wife, as soon as he was born, wrote to me saying that she released me from all the bonds of family life, and gave me full permission to renounce. The relation between husband and wife ceased, and pure unselfish friendship remained. With great happiness I took her at her word and gave her my blessing. I went to pay her a visit and to see my most beloved son at Poona. We all met, had our say, and with a buoyant heart I departed. A heavy burden was lifted from my brain. This I thought was freedom to soar high into the sky, and my wings became stronger in anticipation.

The joy of my parents knew no bounds. They were very happy. Alas, after five months the news came that my son had breathed his last. What a terrible shock for my wife and my parents. I did not feel anything and could hardly afford to spare a tear for the departed soul. My gratitude for him—for it was his birth that gave me my freedom—poured all my tears out before my Lord, and nobody on earth was able to claim a share in them.

I wrote to my father at Amraoti saying that I wanted to be free, that my wife had given me my freedom, and I requested him and my mother to give it to me as well. They desired to see me, and I could not refuse. We met and we talked at length. All the problems of worldly life were solved. His landed property was in his hands now, and free from any litigation. I promised him that as I would not claim anything for myself, my share in his property could go to my younger brother. He told me: "I have done my duty as a householder, given you education, seen that my daughters married, and the only remaining anxiety for the education of my younger son is now over, as you are willing to shoulder that responsibility. I will now die in peace." He knew that I would fulfil my promise, for he had abundant faith in me.

One day we were pacing the fields at Badnera, and my father asked me whether he would see me any more. I said if God desired it, we should meet. He was overwhelmed with feeling, and rushed into the very temple of Lord Shiva where he had offered thanks years before for the birth of a religious son. I remained outside and knew that I was fulfilling the Lord's decree and the wish of my father. My father came out relieved, and after a few days I left for Mount Girnar.

My master was already there. He was glad that I was free from all my religious duties. I was never happier in my life. My misgivings over marriage were at an end. How grateful I felt, and with a full heart wept and prayed to Him who had been all mercy. My efforts had been as nothing compared with His grace in delivering me.

In the beginning, steeped in ignorance and far from knowledge of Him, I had heard Him call. He then gave sufficient strength to pursue the path and to solve the problems of life, as if mine had been His. For love knows no difference between mine and thine, and His love was now mine.

To be a servant is a good touchstone of spiritual life. A man may be willing to give money, to give much of his time to others, but not his body like a slave. Egoism always stands in the way. That is why many saints undergo a rigorous period of personal service. My master loved me, always looked after my comforts first, praised any good action, and forgot to chide me for mistakes. He accepted with perfect cheerfulness whatever was offered. This was not service in a strict sense, but only a first lesson.

My master said: "What is yoga? Yoga is skill in action, as the Lord Shrikrishna says in His *Geeta*.". As he spoke I suspected what was in store for me. The greatness of yoga lies in application of life. Only by serving a man who neither loved nor respected me, who was thoroughly worldly and yet thought himself a holy person, could I learn the meaning of service. The idea was not without its romance, and appealed to my ambition.

I took a place as an ordinary servant on a mere pittance per month, and one meal a day, full time and no luxuries. I brought my wife with me and she also served as an ordinary servant in the household. The children were with us, and food and raiment for them were included in the terms. Thus began my third stage in life, Vanaprastha, or the preparation for complete renunciation.

I was managing the business of my employer from morning till midnight; a terrible task which taught me what real hardship meant. The Sanskrit verse says: "The religion of service is extremely difficult; even for great yogis." I was cashier, accountant, clerk, supervisor, manager and porter. There was no question of appreciation for whatever was well done, my employer took the credit; but failure was always due to me. This is the real power of money; in that world virtue adheres to wealth; a beggar like me has none. A rich man is supposed never to lie or commit sin. Riches is knowledge, riches is virtue, riches is power, riches is divinity, and the man without riches is a brute and deserves to be kicked. He does not deserve to live in this world at all. Such is the theory of wealth.

My concern was not with humiliation or indignity, but with service and love. To love a man incapable of reciprocating the feeling is walking on fire, and to me fell the honour of attempting it. My master helped me in my ordeal. He was in the thick of the fight, guarding me, helping me and giving me his spiritual consolation.

The Ordeal of Service

I had no knowledge of this world. Now I began to learn. Thank Heaven for giving me a chance of seeing the other side of things. I was associated with my employer to such an extent that people marvelled; how could they understand? Few understand spiritual trials. "Once a friend, always a friend", was my motto. Disinterested service was my watchword. Now in spite of sincere efforts, I gave satisfaction to no single soul. To convince anybody of your motives is very difficult. Your task is to convince yourself, and act with God in your heart and God overhead.

That I did, and came successfully through after four years' trial; then I gave notice and left. My wife and children went to the ashram of my master, and I went to Bombay.

24

Go Back, My Child

THE hardships of service had exhausted my body, which was undermined by influenza and malaria till a railway journey shook it so as to bring on fever. But, as Lord Dattatreya willed, as soon as I reached Bombay, an old College friend of mine met me accidentally, pushed me into his car and took me to his palatial house on the Malabar Hill. He and his wife nursed me till I gradually recovered. As the summer approached, we went to Mahabaleshwar, the summer hill station of the Government of Bombay.

My master was there as an honoured guest, so I had the privilege of serving him again. We walked five or six miles in the hills every morning, and sometimes in the evening again; our steps were measured by our meditation on the name and form of our Lord. We wore European suits; very few knew us, and so we were not troubled by callers. We had no cares, and this happy time lasted for two months wherein I lived on wisdom from my master's lips. My physical strength returned and I put on weight. At last, having decided to visit Mount Girnar, I distributed my little possessions among the few friends I was leaving. None of them guessed my purpose except one young man, who gave me a pilgrim's gown. Off I started with this and a brass pot to hold water. I owned enough to buy a ticket as far as Junagadh, and a kindly lady gave me a rupee for refreshments.

I had vowed to give myself, body, mind and soul, to Lord Dattatreya, but not a body weakened with disease and hard usage, so I had restored it to its full vigour that it might be a worthy gift. July is the most terrible month on Mount Girnar. Thunder and lightning and ceaseless rain force folk to keep the doors shut, or clouds of fog invade the house and wet everything. Wild beasts roam the vicinity; the pilgrimage is interrupted; even the priests retreat to the city at the foot of the mountain, save a few who inside their temples crouch over braziers to keep themselves warm.

In this weather I set out for the hills, a rag of cloth round my loins, my *kamandalu* in my hand. With more clothing the gusts would have hurled me into the ravines beneath. The fog hid everything but a bare yard of the path in front of me. The water came cascading down the steps to meet me or flushed round my ankles in a descent as a torrent round the piers of a bridge. The danger of slipping was great and constant. Beautiful wild flowers peeped up through sopped grass to relieve the eye. Handsome serpents sped on their zigzag way and showed no desire to make friends with me. Not a soul was to be seen.

One day a big cobra was crossing the path before me; our eyes met; it tried to retire to the covert from which it had issued. The right to cross the path first is his, I thought, ashamed that it should fear me. Then mentally I admonished it: "Well, sir, push on; yours is the right, you started first. Your dread of me insults my spirituality. I am the last person to think of hurting you." He would not stir but waited for me to pass on. We stood still for a couple of minutes; then, to my joy, the cobra pursued its journey. It made a lovely sight and kept looking back till it gained the covert across the road. A watchman wondered why I stood there like a statue, hurried to me, and when I told him about the cobra, he would have followed and dispatched it. I held him fast and told him that I would not allow him to; the snake was my friend—I had seen love in its eyes, and owed my life to its kindness. He was dumbfounded. I admit that it is difficult to realise the divine unity of life in practice, but failure to do so entails harder trials in lives we have yet to live. The significance of eternal life can only be realised here and now by those who are ready to take any risk rather than fail in sympathy. We must be wedded to eternity no matter at what cost, and only love wins love.

At times the heavy majestic roar of the lion was heard through the pelting of the rain, and in spite of the rumbling clouds and the screaming of birds; these sounds with the density of the fog exerted a kind of fascination. With measured steps, in meditation, the name of the Lord on my lips, I pushed my way towards the solitary peak on which the Lord has left the print of His feet.

I bathed in Kamandalu Teertha, the sacred pool, and filled my brass pot, and, plucking a few flowers, pressed on to the summit; kneeling before the marks, touching them with my forehead, and pouring the sacred water over them, I repeated the Upanishads and the other Sanskrit and Marathi hymns. Though my body had been losing strength, the growing purity of my mind supported it. Like scars that heal, the evil obsessions left in my mind by my four years of servitude faded out under the influence of the penance I was undergoing.

I passed the nights in a damp cabin, lying on a woollen carpet with a small blanket to cover me, shivering with cold which kept me wide awake to remember His name, and prevent my wasting time in sleep. Towards the end, renouncing my daily portion of milk, I lived only on water.

Day after day I climbed the Lord's peak. When weakness came over me, I prayed and automatically received new strength. Even the water-pot became at last too heavy for me; the holy tank was reached with more and more difficulty, till once after my bath, lifting the full *kamandalu* I suddenly fell and remember the sound of the brass vessel on the pavement, as, straining with both hands against the ground, I vomited. There was nobody to hear my voice, and consciousness left me. When my eyes reopened, my limbs were benumbed and darkness was thickening all round. The effort to get on to my tottering feet made me fear it impossible to reach the peak. But prayer was answered, and, refreshed by another bath, I climbed five hundred steps, repeating the Sadguru Upanishad. My success filled me with elation.

Next morning at Junagadh my friends welcomed me back. I had given the whole strength of my mature body to the Lord in its full vigour, not taxed by disease; He had accepted sinew and flesh and returned me in their stead the flame of His spirit burning more brightly than ever.

All glory to Him!

25

I know Him too well!

I THEN returned to my master at his ashram and stayed there till the anniversary of Lord Shrikrishna. A few friends of his gathered to offer their prayers to the Lord and their obeisance to my master. All sang the Upanishads, and the prayers in Sanskrit, Hindi or Marathi; the whole atmosphere was surcharged with spiritual life, and we all found relief from the worries and anxieties of the world. They came with flowers and fruit for our master, and offered him *dakshina* (free-will money offerings) before they departed. He was at his best, and we succeeded in drawing him out on some of the essential characters of spiritual life.

My master's joy in celebrating the anniversary of Lord Dattatreya knew no bounds. To listen to wonderful accounts of the esoteric life of this universe, which is a sealed book to ordinary people, was our good fortune. His actions and sayings were often too deep for me, but I had faith in his ability to explain the most abnormal mystery when the time should be ripe. Impatience to forestall comprehension I found only delayed it.

My next ordeal was to live alone on the top of the Tungarli Hills, in a small cabin on the bank of the reservoir which supplies water to Lonavala. Many friends warned me that a tiger had been recently shot and his mate was prowling the hills, athirst for vengeance. "I am not afraid of her; she has no need to fear me", was my reply. One friend furnished the cabin with a small cot, a chair, a table and writing material. The watchman who came up daily to sound the water at 10 A.M. brought me three pounds of butter-milk. He was my only visitor.

Spring was fast approaching, and Nature assumed her most gorgeous attire. The atmosphere was sweet with fragrant wild flowers. Occasionally I met the deadliest cobras; of a night I heard

8. Prem Nivas at Tapovan Ashram, Lawasha (Photograph by Vinod Sena).

the roar of the maddened tigress. Once during my meditation a serpent found its way indoors and kept dashing its hood against the wall. There was only a distance of six inches between us when it turned; I got up and opened the door for it. On another occasion when I was about to lie down, a scorpion was creeping under my pillow. "If it is His will that this creature should bite me, there is no power on earth which can prevent it. If it is not His will, why trouble?" Before long I was fast asleep.

The fear of wild animals is largely imaginative. We need much persuading before we relinquish habits so vividly impressed on childhood. My father had early undermined in me the nursery panic at serpents. Those who set too high a value on life ignore that before this life they have had many and are destined to be born again and again, after this life has been taken from them. The present is a small sacrifice for that union with eternal being only to be attained by selfless sympathy, by an absorption that counts no cost.

The birds were my best company. Seated on a slab of stone, loudly singing the Sadguru Upanishad in praise of Lord Dattatreya, I watched the sun slowly set. The Great Artist was painting; the picture grew and altered, and the birds who a second before were chirping so noisily, had apparently taken the vow of silence and were listening to my song. Another evening I did not feel inclined to sing, and the birds continued their songs so late as to jar on my desire for silence; they, however, came out from the bushes and frisked and played and delighted my eyes. Then, when at last I began to sing the Upanishads for joy, they hurried back to their nests and became silent. Evening after evening I experimented; desirous of watching their play I kept silent, sitting still as a statue, till they ventured to perch on my body—once even a nightingale from the summit of my head poured forth her music. If I wanted them to go to bed, to chant the sacred hymns was the signal. Love and fellowship reigned between us, for I had not a single grain of rice with which to allure them.

My fame spread far and wide as though I were a Mahatma. Rich people came to Lonavala in the spring and wanted to have a sight of the man who lived on butter-milk alone in the hills. But hating to

The Autobiography of an Indian Monk

be disturbed, I locked my door of a morning and returned home only after dusk, passing all the day in the thickness of the forest.

One day I chanced on some students, who seized me, persuaded me to accompany them to the town, put on the dress of a gentleman, eat with them, play at ping-pong, badminton and cricket, and be happy in the little pleasures of friendliness. All praised the Mahatama who lived on the Tungarli Hills and asked if I had met him there. "Oh yes, I know him only too well!" was my reply, given in all seriousness.

26

The Begging-Bowl

By 1923, I had completed the three stages of spiritual training: Brahmacharya, or celibacy; Grihasta-Ashram, or the duties of a householder; and Vanaprastha, or the preparation for complete renunciation. This last had been done at the ashram of my master, where I had worked as a bricklayer, carpenter and cowherd, sowing rice or picking in the sugar-fields, and occasionally assisting in the temple, or taking the part of the priest in charge. This severe training had lasted for nine months, and it was high time that the fourth stage of my life should begin: Sannyasa-Ashram, or complete renunciation.

The worldly ties of family and social life were slackening fast, and the spiritual life became ever more dominant. My master one day summoned me, and asked me to go to Mount Girnar and thence on pilgrimage throughout the length and breadth of India. I was to pay my respects to the four great monasteries: Dwarka, Jagannath Puri, Rameshwaram and Badrinath, founded by the philosopher, saint and prophet Shri Shankaracharya, who lived nearly twelve hundred years ago, and also the seven *puris* or cities,[1] the twelve sacred shrines of Lord Shiva,[2] the four of the Goddess Jagadamba[3] (or the Mother of the Universe), and all those dedicated to Lord Dattatreya,[4] and any others that lay on the road. I was to obey the

---

[1] That is: Avantika (Ujjain), Ayodhya, Mathura, Haridwar, Kashi (Varanasi), Kanchi and Dwarika. *Editor.*

[2] The Dwadash Jyotirling cover: Shri Vishwanath (Kashi), Vaidyanath Dham (Devdhar, Bihar), Shri Shail Mallikarjuna (Deccan), Rameshwaram, Triambakesvara (Nasik), Somnath, Omkaresvara (Rajasthan), Hatkesvara (Junagadh), Mahakalesvara (Ujjain), Dhrishnevara (Ellora), Nagesh (Maharashtra). *Editor.*

[3] The temples of Kamakhya (Guwahati), Meenakshi (Madurai), Jwala Devi (Kangra) and Kamadani (Kamkoti, Deccan). *Editor.*

[4] Besides Mt. Girnar, Varanasi, Mahur and Narsoba Wadi, mentioned by Purohit

following rules:
1. To beg my food in the name of the Lord, but only once a day.
2. To accept for this meal any invitation, no matter from whom it came.
3. To act without any observance of caste or limitation by creed or status.
4. Never to beg for money or garments.
5. To change my bed and hosts everyday unless invited to remain.
6. To accept cooked food only.

He gave me the begging-bowl and his blessing, and I departed for Mount Girnar and climbed the Lord's peak in gratitude for His having freed me from all worldly worries and for accepting me into His sacred order.

My master had told my mother, on their first meeting sixteen years before, that his happiness would be full when he should see her son set out with a begging-bowl. Whatever food was offered was accepted with gratitude, for it came from my Divine Master. Men who gave it merely acted as His agents. Often it was injurious to my health, yet it was sent by Him and my beloved friend and therefore eaten with relish.

I lived in a small hut in the Raiji's gardens. The first night my carpet was devoured by white ants, so I went to a paved terrace and slept for three nights on the stone. Extremely beautiful the place was, secluded from the bustle of city life. My programme was carried out with regularity. To beg for my food, I went to the city at noon, and remained to talk with my hosts on spiritual matters if they were so inclined. Once a high official invited me, and after our talk insisted on taking me back to the garden in his carriage. When he found that I had not even a carpet, with tears in his eyes he sent there and then for a frame bed stretched with bands of canvas woven together, and a new rug, saying: "There are millions whose night's rest is comfortably provided for, and here I find a man who might be an ornament to the Bombay bar lying uncovered on stone flags!"

Swami, the places sacred to Dattatreya would include: Sage Atri's hermitage on the Godavari, Pithapura, Kurvapura, Gokarna, Gangapura, Triambakeṣvara, Kolhapur, Auravadi, Bhilwadikumasi, Mallikarjuna, Karanjapura, etc. *Editor.*

The Begging-Bowl

In India many thousands beg in the name of God at the houses of married people, and teach in return the wisdom they have realised. The Hindu scriptures have enjoined on all householders the duty of giving food to any sanyasin or monk who appeals to them. So throughout the country the principles of spirituality are frequently expounded among both rich and poor. An Englishman asked me whether all these sadhus, fakirs or monks were not a burden to society. I urged that the fee or tax was voluntary and the benefit received at once in the shape of theory or exhortation or narrative. The results of the highest development of the human faculties in privately endowed ashrams were in the most human and gracious manner diffused equally through all classes in proportion to the individual's readiness to welcome them. Life was quickened and increased, and yet not embarrassed by notions and information that the recipients were not ripe enough to digest. If a few individuals take advantage of these customs, what other establishments cost less or achieve more for the sanctification of life!

The vast Indian continent is a conglomeration of so many races and sects which, though culturally the same, yet differ widely, in their customs, languages, dress, diet and conduct. Since I had no personal aims left, I could the more easily approach all whom I met or received hospitality from. Today I fed at the house of a man who hailed from Deccan; tomorrow I dined with a man born and bred in Gujrath; the third day a man from Kathiawar invited me. The fashion of hospitality differed, but each was as welcome as any other, for all were offered to me by my Divine Friend. I studied the varied modes of living in order to convey my message to everyone in a style that would suit his ways of thinking. This was no easy task, but success in it would realise the full significance of the title, "Swami." Old-fashioned people, who used the language of the Vedas and Upanishads, failed to grasp the new thought and style, and the half-Westernised failed to understand those of the sacred books. In the shadow of Mount Girnar I learnt the alphabet of spiritual life from pilgrims of every condition and language, while walking the streets with my begging-bowl.

Spring had begun! I passed the hot days and the pleasant nights in the gardens. Hundreds of roses cascaded over tree and shrub, filling the air with their fragrance. Among mango trees in bloom the cuckoo called; beautiful peacocks danced in front of me; bees were humming, and nobody came to fret my peace. I went to the town for my meal and passed the remainder of the day in meditation, prayer and reading the *Bhagwat* by Shri Eknath Swami, who lived three hundred years ago. This book contains the philosophy of devotion and was a standard to measure my life against, as it has been for thousands of Indians. Within it we find the gospel of Lord Shrikrishna as preached to his first and foremost disciple, Shri Uddhava Swami, five thousand years ago, the inspiration of many great saints and prophets.

Too many changes of diet, too many heavy foods told on my health. The summer became very hot, and I decided to continue the pilgrimage planned by my Master. The day before my departure the Prime Minister of a State in Kathiawar and I met in the house of a friend. He vehemently condemned my attitude of renunciation, and when he learned I planned to go to the Himalayas, he asked me whether I had sufficient money. "I start next day", was my reply, "and have not a farthing. Should I in the meantime receive money, the journey will be by rail, otherwise I walk." I went away, giving him my blessing. The next day he came to give me two rupees, and I told him smilingly that he answered his own question. I was met by another gentleman who took me to his place for a meal, and gave me a few more rupees and then settled me in a comfortable compartment with a second-class ticket for Rajkot.

On the evening of my arrival there, proposing to lodge with a friend, I asked a lady who was standing at the door of her house with her baby in her arms, to direct me. She said she could not show me the way as it was getting dark and her children must have their meal, but she was expecting her husband back and he would show me. As her husband was late, I decided to have my bath, which was nearly finished when the owner of the house entered. Seeing me, he frowned. So I told him my story. He began abusing me. How dared I renounce this world and enter his house without his permission? It was evident where his shoe pinched him. I listened calmly for over an hour until he went inside to his wife. When he returned he overflowed in apologies, and asked whether I had been angry. "Had I been, you would no longer have found me here." Meanwhile my friend arrived and led me to his home. When he learnt the whole story, he laughed, for he had known that gentleman's anger.

27

I am Dattatreya

OFTEN when I wanted to leave for a new destination and made enquiries about the journey, someone would buy me a ticket, by third, by second or first class, or even for the saloon. When I had to journey by road, a bullock-cart, horse-carriage or a motor-car would offer me a lift, or if not, my feet served me. To learn a total dependence upon the divine will, I had to free my mind of all concern about food, money or shelter for the night. Why should Providence interfere if I busied myself about such things!

I went from Rajkot to Delhi, making short stays at some of the important places of pilgrimage like Puskaraj, which is the only place where Brahmadeo, or the God of Creation, is worshipped, and is therefore much visited from all parts of India. On nearing Delhi, a rich man came from his compartment and asked me where I should put up. "I do not know," I said, and that surprised him. He repeated the question, but got no definite information. This made him angry, so he returned to his seat, saying: "You are a sadhu, and yet tell me a lie! You must know where you are to put up." His view was understandable and amused me. But the incident put me off my guard; and I began to plan: many people had spoken of the Maharashtra Mandal, so I resolved to go there. The train stopped at Delhi, and taking my *kamandalu*, I started on my way; but the guard of the train placed his hand on my shoulder. He saluted and said: "Swamiji, it is now midday. Everyone will be gone to business at this late hour. Can you wait a few minutes, while I finish my duty, and then accompany me to my poor cottage? I shall feel highly honoured." It was my duty to accept all invitations, so I welcomed his hospitality, inwardly humiliated at having given thought to that which God had ordered wonderfully well.

A friend sent me to Kurukshetra, where Lord Shrikrishna preached the *Geeta* to his favourite disciple, Prince Arjuna. I worshipped the Lord for bringing me to a place honoured by all Hindus, and for entrusting me to the servant of my friend who was then looking after all my needs. Thence I went to Hardwar, at the foot of the Himalayas, where the sacred river Ganges is worshipped by thousands of pilgrims every year. Hundreds of sadhus and sanyasins were there. It was joy to be at the foot of the sacred range, to penetrate into the heart of which had been the dream of my life.

From Hardwar to Rishikesh, a horse-carriage gave me a lift, and lodging was offered in a *dharmashala*, one of those guest-houses which are to be seen throughout India, especially on routes of pilgrimage. The sadhus may stay in them free of all charge. About a thousand sanyasins are lodged at the Anna-Chhatram foundation, where they receive sufficient bread and curry to keep body and soul together. I could not go there as my rule forced me to beg for each day's needs. At first this caused surprise among them, but after a few days they got to know me, and invited me for meals. I visited various sanyasins, and was much interested to gain insight into their spiritual lives. Some were highly educated, some were pious men who could neither read nor write.

The climate was rigorous, extremely hot by day and extremely cold by night. One day I received too much food, and the next too little. These irregularities weakened me and I caught fever. A learned professor from the United Provinces came and showed great concern; he gave me much praise, and everyone thought he had made himself responsible for my needs. Nothing of the kind, he merely bored me with talk which it was my difficult duty to suffer with toleration while lying on my carpet in high fever. Though taking baths regularly in the icy-cold water of the Ganges, I was too weak to wander begging for food. The professor offered me nothing except a daily cup of tea. At last, despite the fever, I walked to Laxman Zula, had a bath, worshipped at the shrine and paid my respects to the various sadhus who were there, and started back to Rishikesh. My feverish, tottering steps missed the path in the darkness; someone took my hand and led me back into the right road. It was only a year later that I learned who this real Mahatma had been.

I am Dattatreya

While walking, I heard two voices vehemently talking. One said that he had seen nearly all the sanyasins at Rishikesh but not one had satisfied him or answered his question. I asked him what it was, and at once satisfied him. Unfortunately, as I then had over six degrees of fever, the nature of his difficulty has escaped from memory. Touching my feet, he exclaimed, "Are you a Mahatma?" I told him, "No, only a disciple." But he wanted to know more about me, and so he and his friend came that night to see me. Since there was no light both the gentlemen were in fear of scorpions, for which Rishikesh is noted. The rule is that there should be a light in every house and oil can be had free from the Kali Kamliwale Bawa's *math*. My rule forbade me to ask for anything but food, so these gentlemen fetched candles from their homes. At the end of a long talk in reply to their questions, my wish to leave for Kashmere the next morning at ten was avowed, and my lack of money confessed. They promised to give me a few rupees, and we parted.

The next day the superintendent of the place came to offer me a lift from Rishikesh to Hardwar. I was glad for help over fourteen miles of my 1400-mile journey. At 9.50 I left, when one of the two gentlemen came running after me, saying that he had forgotten the hour of my departure and was meditating on the banks of the Ganges when a sanyasin came to him and said: "Well, my boy, you must hurry if you mean to give the Swami what you promised." He asked the sanyasin his name, and he replied, "I am Dattatreya", and then disappeared. The gentleman left everything, ran to his house, and came to me with five rupees in his hand. I explained with tears in my eyes who Dattatreya was, and got into my carriage, abashed that the Lord had had to take so much trouble for me.

I went thence to Amritsar, where a wealthy Sikh accommodated me in his house, paid my respects to the Golden Temple, and met various of these sadhus; then to Lahore, to see my friend who had invited me. He received me very cordially in his shop, and sent word to his wife about my arrival. We talked for some time there, and then went to his house. My room was on the fourth floor, and his wife brought me dishes of her own making; but all the duties of full hospitality could not disguise that her smile was forced. She fell at my feet, and I gave her blessings in the name of the Lord; when

I asked her about her children, she said they had already gone to bed.

My friend sat up with me nearly all night. His servants fanned me, for it was very hot; yet something seemed strained in the house. I rose at 4 A.M., and my friend greeted me with joy, saying that all was due to me. I did not understand what he meant, till with tears of gratitude in his eyes he told me that the previous evening five eminent doctors had examined his eldest daughter and son, and said that all would be over before daybreak; in spite of this he and his wife had welcomed me as if nothing was the matter. During the night the children's temperatures fell to normal, and now the doctor said they were out of danger. I told him that it was not my doing, but my Divine Master's, and it was therefore to Him that gratitude was due.

When I remonstrated with his wife for serving me with so much rich food, she only said: "I am a Hindu wife, and it is my duty to offer the best that I have to a Swami, who represents the highest spiritual life in the world. I have but obeyed the rules of hospitality as given by my religion. There is nothing dearer to me than my faith and my God."

28

Another Temptation

I BEGGED for food alone, yet one day I resolved to leave for Kashmere on the morrow. My host, who had taken his doctor's degree in England, asked me how the journey was to be made without money. "Wait and see," was my reply. My departure was fixed. At 1 A.M. a learned Pandit gave me five rupees; an hour later another man presented me a second five rupees, and so on till at 7 A.M. I had twenty-one rupees, sufficient for a ticket to Jammu, and to pay for an omnibus from there to Shrinagar.

The omnibus was prevented from starting by a gentleman stepping from a private car and saying: "Salutations to you, Swamiji." Being in overcoat and balaclava cap, I suppose he could not be addressing me, but he came, touched my feet and repeated: "Salutations to you, Swamiji. You think I do not recognise you, but you remember the Astrologer Royal to His Highness the Maharaja of Kashmere." Then I had to return his salutations and enquired where he was going. "Shrinagar," he answered, then asked me where I meant to stay. "I do not know." He smiled and said we were sure to meet again soon. Every passenger in the omnibus knew the Astrologer Royal, and throughout the journey they treated me with the greatest courtesy and kindness.

At Shrinagar, putting up in the Shri Shankaracharya monastery, visitors began to gather round me, for I begged for a meal every day at a new house. Nor was it long before a great official invited me to take up my lodging in one of his houses, and bade his servants to look after me. Spring in the "earthly paradise" revels in millions of flowers. The Jhelum sweeps majestically, swollen by the melting Himalayan snows; everybody worships the sun or bathes or is out boating on Lake Dal. Here Sanskrit learning had once reached its apogee and still retains something of its former lustre, though against the odds. Plain living and high thinking is the motto of the various Brahmin Pandits whom I met, and something of the pristine glory of Aryan spiritual civilisation is found surviving among their families.

The rooms allotted to me proved to have windows in which half the glass was broken, and offered no protection from the glacial winds and long cold nights; but a sanyasin must not complain of his entertainment. My host knew nothing of my sufferings. He sent me food every night, but the Mohammedan servant who brought the dish took practically the whole of its contents for himself, for he was dying of hunger. Yet his intervention between his master and myself often amused me, and I found some compensation for the pangs of hunger in the garden glorious with flowers. At night, with knees drawn up under my stomach, my back like a vaulted roof over the little warmth I could hold together, the repetition of the Lord's name brought me peace if not sleep, till a pair of nightingales ushered in the morning with singing to one another from broken window to window across my room and made me company.

A pleader in the Courts, meeting me, bareheaded, gave four rupees to furnish me with a turban. A gold-bordered one was offered; this I refused, but the shop-man in turn refused to take it back and wanted to return the money to my benefactor, and with difficulty was persuaded to keep the money on condition that I wore the gaudy headdress. Many had to wonder that a Swami carrying a begging-bowl should wear such a turban, golden shoes and a fine overcoat. All these things had come to me from my Beloved One, and I accepted them with gratitude. Renunciation is not an outward condition, but a temper of mind which people recognise however disguised.

One day my meal was laid before me at an exalted official's table with all pomp and ceremony; the next, in a poor beggar's hut, it consisted of rice and curry served on a lotus leaf under the shade of a chinar tree in a furious dust-storm, so that I had to make my body a pent-house over the dish and swallow the food as quickly as possible before it became too gritty. These frequent and violent changes in the amount and quality of food, added to the extremities of cold which I suffered every night, soon made me ill. Nor would my rules suffer me to ask for medicines nor allow me to refuse

Another Temptation

unsuitable diet. The Astrologer Royal was very kind to me, and understood the causes of my sorry plight. He prophesied to me one day; "Swami, as yet nobody knows you, but in two years' time you will go forth on your spiritual mission recognised by all." As the reader will see, these words came true in due course.

I next visited at Achchabal the spiritual preceptor of the late Maharaja of Kashmere. After a night in a free travellers' bungalow I went to pay my respect to Shri Santdeo Swami at a two-roomed cottage in the jungle. He was resting on a couch and leisurely smoking his hookah when I entered. He recognised me and instructed his private secretary, who was sitting at his feet, to attend to my comforts. We had much lively conversation on spiritual matters. He noticed that I looked run down and wanted to telegraph to His Highness and arrange for my further pilgrimage by car. To me this seemed another dangerous temptation, so the next day I asked the Swami to give me leave to depart. He would not hear of it and detained me for another day by saying: "How can you go unless you first partake of our Kashmere rice pudding? Impossible!" This was an invitation to dinner which must not be refused. After enjoying the meal on the following day, I heard the Swami bid his secretary remind him about the telegram before he went to take his siesta. I determined to run away. A pilgrimage is not to be made in royal state when, as mine was, it is a penance. So I packed my few possessions and, leaving a message with the secretary both of excuse and profuse thanks, hurried back to Shrinagar.

Though my pockets were as empty as ever a few days later, I resolved to start for Lahore and was trudging the road with my *kamandalu* and a small blanket, when a Pandit asked me whither I was bound, and then introduced me to an Englishman, asking him to give me a lift in a car he had hired as far as Murree. He gladly accepted my company, for he was alone. We talked on various spiritual themes in which he happened to be much interested. It was nearly 4 P.M. when he asked if I had any objection to partaking of a cup of coffee and biscuits at the next dak bungalow. I said that the refreshment would be most welcome. Then he asked whether I had had any breakfast. I did not answer. Straightaway he told the chauffeur to return to the last dak bungalow we had passed, and with a thousand apologies ordered milk and biscuits for me. He asked how it was I had had no breakfast, and was extremely surprised to learn the nature of my vows. We reached Murree in the evening, and with a blessing I took leave of him and went into a travellers' bungalow.

A learned Pandit, my fellow-lodger there, gave me a lift in his car as far as Rawalpindi the next morning, and took a ticket for me to Lahore, whence, after a few days, I went on to Delhi and thence to Muttra,[1] the sacred place where Lord Shrikrishna lived, which, having long desired to see, I was overjoyed to visit.

[1] Mathura. *Editor.*

29

My Lord Shrikrishna

EAGER to reach the sacred place Muttra, I journeyed all day so as to have time, since it was Thursday and therefore sacred to Lord Dattatreya, to visit the various temples and pray in them before begging for my meal. To see the places where the events of Lord Shrikrishna's life had taken place, rejoiced and uplifted me. My feet paced the sacred ground which the Lord had trodden five thousand years before. Only a devotee of God can understand my emotion as each episode was recalled by the scene wherein it had been enacted. Entranced I wandered the city till 10 P.M., then approached a priest to beg for food. He coldly told me to go to the market and buy some *puries* (biscuits) and vegetables, and pointed the way. I had but one penny left; with it I bought some mouthfuls and was sitting on Jumna's banks with it still in my hands when a pack of monkeys gathered round me claiming their share. I hurriedly took a few morsels, then as in duty bound gave them the remainder, drank the river water from my hands, muttered my prayer, and went to take my rest.

The second day I went to Brindavan, the sacred place where the Gopees, the women cowherds of Gokul, worshipped the Lord, and enjoyed the supreme bliss in His company. Pilgrims from all parts of the country roll themselves on the earth where the Lord set His blessed feet. More tears are shed in adoration for God in Brindavan than in any other place. The great devotees sing His praises day and night, and yearn for a vision of Him. Holy Krishna is Lord of rich and of poor, virtuous and sinning, learned and ignorant; did He not cry: "Come one, come all; the way is open!" He preached the gospel of love, and for His sake thousands of Indians have sacrificed their nearest and dearest. Here Shri Mirabai rebuked a sadhu who boasted that he would never look on a woman, and whenever he left the monastery kept his eyes on the ground, with "Lord Shrikrishna alone was a man, compared with Him all others are women", and humbled him.

A little farther was where the Lord danced with His disciples and tested their love, and just beyond that He played on His flute, and the people went mad with the sound of it; nay, even cows and birds were beside themselves. Many a tear of gratitude watered each spot, many a prayer to Him was sighed from the humility of my heart. As every act of His was recalled to mind, trees, the descendants of those under whose shade He once sat, were embraced, the Jumna which had been His bath, became mine, and where He had sat on the bank listening to the songs of birds, I cast my mind back thousands of years to picture Him warmed by the same sun, and when the moon rose whose lovely light had honoured His more lovely features, I seemed to hear the divine flute He had played to her. His presence was with me, eternal life enveloped mine, and mine was merging into His.

At midday I rose to beg for food, wandering listlessly, when a door was opened and an old lady came out. I begged of her. She asked me to wait in the road. The door was open, and within I saw a beautiful young lady in a silk *sari* spinning at her wheel. Our eyes met, she folded her hands and saluted me, and I gave her my blessings in return. Her mother-in-law came back with some *puries* and said: "Swamiji, you will not mind though they are stale? They remain over from the offerings to God!" I saluted her, saluted the food in my hand, and began to eat with a cheerful countenance. She then asked if I would like some pickles, and they, too, were stale remnants of an offering. I ate with relish. She brought me more, but the daughter-in-law intervened: "Please do not give those *puries* to the Mahatma. Even a dog would not eat them. There is fresh food in the house, why not share it with him?" But the mother chid her with a stern look, and thrust some more stale *puries* into my hand which, being extremely hungry, I ate gladly. Then the old woman poured water into my joined hands that I might drink. I gave her my blessing and thanked her for her kindness. Her old heart melted, her daughter-in-law stood beside her remonstrating, and I was soon aware she was following me: "I am sorry, Swamiji," she was saying, "I treated you very rudely. You are a true devotee born of

My Lord Shrikrishna

a noble family." I replied: "Whether I am noble or pauper, God led me to your door, and you fed me in honour of Him. Having had my meal, I need nothing more." As I parted from her, I saw the beautiful daughter-in-law standing at the door with tears in her eyes.

The next day I set out for Gokul, where Lord Shrikrishna lived as a child. As I crossed the Jumna, I repeated to myself the songs of great poets in Sanskrit, Marathi and Hindi who celebrate His life. At this very ford Vasudeo, His father, bore the sacred infant across and had to lift Him higher and higher, for the devout waters of the river piled themselves up to reach and kiss His little feet, and when at last they had done so they subsided on the instant that they might not hinder His passage. But now their surface remained smooth and without a ripple. No cloud, no wind, though this was the very heart of the rainy season. The outward peace was so great that my heart ached as though something were missing.

Alighting from the ferry, I visited the sacred places in Gokul and returned to the river-bank and looked all about me. "Everything is calm," I exclaimed to myself. "Here is Gokul, but where is that Jumna noted for her boisterous waves? Where are the clouds which poured with rain when the Lord was born? Where is the lightning that flashed when Vasudeo brought the child from Muttra? Where the fierce wind? Where the rain? the thunder? I have come here, but see none of these. My heart burns to see the same sights as were then seen. Let me close my eyes on these tears and pray." Standing on the bank, with folded hands, this petition escaped me: "I must see! I will not move unless I see!"

After reflection, my thoughtless blunder roused me to bitter repentance; but I, like the old lady who offered me fresh food when I had dined off stale, was too late, my first prayer was already answered. The heavens were pitch dark, the thunder rolled around, and within fifteen minutes of my reaching that spot, torrents of rain fell; the Jumna grew boisterous, the lightning flashed, the wind roared, the peacocks danced with joy, and in amazement people ran pell-mell for shelter. Left alone on the bank, my arms folded, I repeated the Upanishads, and watched the ferocious Jumna and her terrifying waves. With cotton gown all sopped, without headgear, I enjoyed the scene for half an hour, then began to shiver with cold, but would not seek a fire. How enchanting! I had prayed for it, and lo! it had come.

After a time the clouds began to disperse, the wind dropped, the Jumna sank into stillness, the birds ventured from their nests to sing once more, and people who had rushed to the fireside heaved a sigh of relief and came out of doors. Though now aglow with gratitude and love. I had sought no shelter. Suddenly a gentleman ran up to me and said: "Swamiji, would you like to go to Muttra? There is a rich man who has engaged a ferry and he would carry you to the other shore. The Jumna is so wonderful! Half an hour ago she was raging, and now see, how calm!" I thanked him for the suggestion, approached the ferry, and was taken to Muttra. A gentleman that evening gave me an elegant meal and treated me with every respect. Such was the will of my Lord Shrikrishna.

30

A New Lease of Life

I LEFT Muttra with a heavy heart. The unceasing flow of pilgrims through temples rich with music and incense, the many sites pregnant with momentoes of Holy Krishna's life, had transported me. Yet His praise is everywhere; weaver-baker-scavenger- gardener- butcher-oilman-saints, even Mohammedan saints, have sung His glory. All castes unite in worship of Him. On the remotest lawns of the mighty Himalayas you will come across a shepherd singing:

Why should I fear in this world?
My Lord Shrikrishna is my Protector!

Salutations, yea, thousands of salutations of Him who has shown us the path!

I went next to Ayodhya, the place where Shri Ramachandra was born. He was a prince, and though driven for fourteen years into exile by a jealous stepmother, yet as dutiful son, affectionate brother, loyal husband, loving father, conscientious king and great yogi, became and remains our Indian example. He was willing to sacrifice for the sake of others his throne and his personal comforts, to live in the forest on herbs and roots, yet he fought with his enemies bravely for the good of the world, and ultimately gave his life for the sake of his subjects.

From there I went to Gaya, and from thence visited the Bodhi tree under which the Lord Buddha received illumination, and so on to Benares. Hindus desire at least once in their lives to visit this holiest-of cities, and think it even more blessed to die there. Foreigners cannot appreciate the spectacle presented by the Temple of Shri Kashi Vishvanath, but this is true of every religion: only those born and bred in their traditions can feel the love they evoke. Ridicule is easy, but sympathy demands considerable effort. Hindus when they have the higher respect for their own traditions respect those of others, nor will they curtail the freedom of another for their own benefit. Every man stands spiritually alone and must obey his own conscience. Our philosophy teaches that freedom for each means freedom for all; and toleration is the psychological flower of a race so disciplined.

Ganges, the sacred Ganges! Thou canst not purify those who have no faith in thy purity. Have faith in a stone, and the stone will speak with you. Otherwise it remains a stone. The whole problem is psychological. Have not the marks of Dattatreya's feet on Mount Girnar spoken to me? Saint Mirabai drank the poison, as a draught of immortality sent by her beloved Lord Shrikrishna, and the juice did not dare to kill her. But pure water drunk by one who believes it to be poison is sure to kill. "Faith rules the Universe", means that everybody thinks himself right. Even for sheer ignorance and egoism this is true, but when our faith is in goodness and helpfulness, it is a thousand times truer.

Multitudes worshipped the Lord in Benares; flowers were offered, bells were rung, incense was burned, the Vedas were chanted, and the whole atmosphere was beautiful with divinity. On the ghats the bathers in unison entoned: "Victory to the Ganges—the mother!"

I went next to Calcutta where Kali, Goddess of Destruction, is adored. I ran to her temple and prostrated myself before her. Bhagwan Ramakrishna Paramahamsa worshipped her as the mother, for out of the destroyed past we are born, by that we are taught and nourished, and we desired freedom from that which can be destroyed in us, so that, having given us life, she at last gives us freedom from that in death. The great porphet of the last century worshipped and in due course realised her.

I went to Dakshineshwar, and Belur monastery and other places associated with the sacred lives of the Mahatma and his great disciple, the Swami Vivekananda, the first exponent of Hindu philosophy to the West, and passed on to Jagannath Puri, noted for the car-festival, where I became the guest of a friend who was then Sessions Judge there. He obtained for me access to the Sacred

Temple, and we enjoyed each other's company and that of other friends who came from Calcutta. My host had been born the same day as myself, with in interval of only three hours, yet he became a judge, and I begged from him as a mendicant!

When I returned to Bombay, influenza was raging furiously, and six to seven hundred people died every day. We were surrounded by death, and I nursed nine patients every day. There was mourning in every house. I did my poor best to wait on my friends, and, thanks to Heaven, all whom I tended were saved, but when I went to Nasik, the disease prostrated me for three weeks. When just able to get on my feet, the physician who attened me told me to rest some days before proceeding on my pilgrimage. I hesitated, but at night in a vision the Lord said to me: "How is it that you listen to others? I have ordered everything." The next morning I started for Doulatabad in the Nizam's dominions, where Shri Janarden Swami was blessed by Lord Dattatreya on the roof of the Fort. The Swami waded into a tank and dissolved his body. Not a trace was found, nor was the water deep enough to conceal it. I was one of thousands of pilgrims extremely glad to be where three centuries ago he passed into peace and where still he is often seen.

The Shri Ghrishneshwar Temple dedicated to Lord Shiva and the Beautiful Ellora caves were next visited, then Shri Nagnath and Shri Parli Vaijanath, and so to Shri Shaila mountain, whither pilgrims climb only once a year. The temple dedicated to Lord Shiva is in the midst of a forest which covers the mountain, so that a radius of twenty-five miles includes no inhabitants save a few wild tribes from whom and from the wild animals the Government protects pilgrims during the holy week. I traversed the forest in the company of a pleader, who asked me to be his father-in-law's guest. I accepted the invitation, but the Receiver of the Temple, his father-in-law, was in no mood to put me up, having a strong dislike for sanyasins. However, he gave me food and bade me choose some corner of the temple to sleep in. I lay down under the shade of a tamarind tree, near a stack of firewood. When he saw me lying there on my carpet, he declared that the wood was infested with serpents, and showed me holes in which they lurked. I replied that, being a monk, I had chosen that place in order to inconvenience nobody. He was helpless, but he asked his servants to clean the corner and fill up the holes with bricks, and I lived there day and night in perfect calm and peace, worshipping morning and evening, bathing in the sacred river Krishna, and begging daily for my meal.

When all the pilgrims had left, followed by the posse of police that protected them, the wild beasts roamed everywhere once more. On our way back my friend and I had to pass a night in a temporary bamboo shelter we tethered his horse as close as we could, but at the roar of the tiger the horse began to shiver. The tank hard by was the only one for miles, so all the creatures came thither during the night to drink. Though we burnt a big log of wood in front of our hut, my friend seemed to despair of his life. The roaring came quite near, but, thank Heaven, nothing untoward happened. After daybreak we left, sending a prayer to the Lord Shiva, the destroyer, who had permitted us to live on.

31

The Dream of the Himalayas

I TRAVELLED on to Shri Balaji, visiting many a beautiful place on the way, and made a rapid excursion to Madurai to pay my respects to the Goddess of Fecundity. The spiritual atmosphere is the same everywhere; rituals, language and images are different; for as the Vedas say: "God is one, but known by many names." Southern India is renowned for temples as vast as cities. These were saved from the ravages of the Moslems by the Mahrattas, and many a Southerner whom I met showed his gratitude towards Shivaji the Great by quoting the lines: "Had there been no Shivaji, everybody would have been forced to accept Mohammedanism."

By Kanchi, Sering-Pattam, I reached Cape Comorin[1] where the Bay of Bengal meets the Arabian Sea—a glorious prospect; then on to Shri Rameshwaram, the temple dedicated to Lord Shiva, whence someone paid my fare back to Bombay. I set out again almost at once for Shri Somnath in Kathiawar, where the sacked and ruined temple moved me to tears. At Dwarka, where Holy Krishna reigned, the temple is extremely beautiful. I prostrated myself where years before Saint Mirabai, touching her forehead to the sacred feet of the image, instantaneously vanished into air. After her marriage she had worshipped Lord Shrikrishna's infancy. Whenever she was alone, the holy child, who had been born upwards of four thousand years earlier, appeared to her and played with her, and in time grew up as though He had been her son, till they played games of dice together with much laughter. The prince, her husband, heard her laughing, talking and dancing with a young man, but when he entered, lo! he found her alone, and she merely said that Holy

---

[1]Seringapatnam and Kanyakumari. *Editor.*

Krishna had visited her. In a jealous rage he decreed that she should drink poison, which she, as it came to her from her Lord, drank gladly as though it were a draught of immortality, and received no harm, but then insisted on leaving her husband and living as a sanyasinee at Benares. When she felt her end approaching, she set out to return to the home temple, followed by a crowd of pilgrims who, when they arrived at Dwarka, entered the temple with her, and saw her touch her brow to the feet of the image, and then saw her no more. Her name has become a household word, and her beautiful songs are sung throughout India. My best salutations to her!

Thence I went to Porebunder, the golden city which Lord Krishna gave to Sudama, his poor friend and fellow-disciple under Sage Sandeepani, in return for a handful of shredded rice. What a joy would it have been to stand by when the pauper embraced his kingly friend!

Once more I received my fare back to Bombay, but was soon off again to Trimbakeshwar, near Nasik, and through Central India to Ujjain, a very, very old city where the master of Lord Shrikrishna lived, and where the Lord served him and his wife, even bringing faggots from the forest on His head to feed their hearth. I revered every trait of His discipleship there, and tried to conform to it when I was in the monastery of my master.

I had now visited all the shrines mentioned by my master, except those in the Himalayas, so once more my steps turned to Rishikesh, where I had been prevented from climbing the Himalayas by high fever and excessive weakness. Once more utterly worn out, I hoped to leave this ailing shattered body not even in the sacred Ganges but in the heart of the Himalayas. At Mussoorie I met a friend who introduced me to a physician from Patiala, who examined me and said to my friend: "Dissuade him from going to the Himalayas, for his spleen and liver are already so damaged that I do not believe he will live more than three days." My friend, however, had great faith in me, and as he knew that my master had ordered me to go, he felt sure of my safe return. Previously, at least half a dozen doctors had advised me to rest and to give up travelling.

Warm clothing, a carpet, a blanket and an overcoat proved far too heavy to carry, so a coolie had to be engaged. Before leaving

The Dream of the Himalayas

Mussoorie, I climbed on the hills every day and found it necessary to regulate every detail of my daily life, in order to give myself a chance of success. With not even enough money to pay the coolie, I started out from Mussoorie.

Every morning rising at 3 A.M., I plodded slowly but surely upwards. To travel in the Himalayas in the early hours is to invite death; for that is when wild beasts come down to drink at the river which our path followed. When I asked my coolie to accompany me, with folded hands he replied: "Swamiji, it is all very well for you to go into the forest in the morning. You are a Swami, who has renounced everything, but I am a householder and I want to go back to my wife and children one day." I respected his view, and set out alone not to lose the precious opportunity for meditation, telling him he would find me at the next village. Should he wait for two days and I not appear, he might take for granted that some beast of the forest had made short work of me, and return to his home. I gave him my money-bag and told him that everything that belonged to me would go to him as a lagacy: my carpet, my blanket, my silk-cotton pillow, and the few clothes packed in my beautiful holdall, and my brass *kamandalu*.

From Rishikesh to go to Jumnotri, the source of the sacred river Jumna, on to Gangotri, the source of the sacred river Ganges, and to Shri Kedarnath and Shri Badri Narayan, is six hundred miles. The route from Mussoorie is very beautiful, and the forests are lovely. The previous year there had been great floods, and bridges, even hanging bridges like the Laxman Zula, had been washed away. Everywhere was strewn the tremendous havoc, so much so that the Government had issued orders that pilgrims should not take the risk this year. Huge landslides had cut communications, and prices had risen.

The greater the difficulty, the greater courage I received to face it. From many places pilgrims were going back, because not even a footpath remained to show them the way. The slopes were so slippery that when it rained they became perilous. I had many a fall, for my shoes with tennis soles would not grip into the mud like iron heels. My whole frame would be so rudely shaken that often it was difficult to rise after a fall. But courage was obedience to my best-beloved.

Everybody that passed me saw the perspiration trickling down my sleeves. Those with some knowledge of medicine pitied me, but their advice was never such as I could take.

The Kali Kamliwale Bawa's monasteries gave me some wheat flour, lentils and potatoes; my coolie cooked for me. I took two *fulkas* or thin cakes prepared by him at 12 A.M., and again two at 8 P.M. before going to bed. From 4 A.M. I climbed the hills till noon, then took a meal, and at 2 P.M. set out on my march till sunset. In my sleep I groaned terribly, my limbs so ached; the coolie felt sorry for me, but I would not allow him to massage me. Several times, having missed my way in the jungle, I found myself once more where I had passed the night. My coolie smiled and said: "Well Swamiji, here you are at last!"

Pilgrims were very kind, though on account of my overcoat, socks and shoes, and balaclava cap, they did not recognise me for a sadhu. Had I worn the orange cloth of a sanyasin, I should have been far better comforted, but I was determined not to take advantage of the Swami's costume for personal ends. Some thought me a prince travelling incognito, others took me for a well-to-do gentleman, very few for the monk that I was.

Each night I found shelter in the *dharmashalas*. At times there was no room left, then I had to lie down under the shade of a tree. The cold was bitter, and the wind fierce. The waters of the rivers were icy, and at times as thick as cream with half-melted snow, yet my bath was never omitted.

One night, rolled in my blanket on a heap of leaves, covered with my carpet, I found something soft lying against my feet, and could not imagine what it might be; at last my feet informed me that it was some animal. When time came to rise, though afraid that it might be a tiger, I repeated the name of God, and got on my legs. The animal leaped up, wagged its tail and licked my hands. After having performed my daily duties and set out, the light of day revealed a dog resembling a leopard, with shaggy hair and a formidable jaw. He followed me peacefully. At the next halt, when my coolie caught me up, he told me that in the night he had been afraid for my life and his own, thinking it a tiger, and had covered his head in the bedclothes. The village folk asked me whether the dog belonged to me, and I said: "Yes, all that is God's is mine, as I am a Swami; but if you think the dog yours, you are free to take him."

These dogs are able to guard a thousand sheep from any wild animal. Even the tiger dares not attack. Every village headman told me that according to custom he must keep the dog fastened up, and send information about, till the real owner came to take it away. But as soon as I started, the dog broke even iron chains, and followed me, a most obedient servant. He had come, nobody could say from whence, but with a purpose which no power on earth seemed able to withhold him from. I owe my life to his protection through those jungles, infested with wild beasts.

With steps regulated by my breathing, and repeating the name of God, my body and mind worked in harmony. They say in India: "Take him who does not believe in God to the range of perpetual snow, and he will understand." If anybody wishes to meditate, sacred footprints of the Mahatmas are there; the words of the Vedas were inspired there; there the *rishis* and sages have seen the great vision, heard the great message, and spoken inestimable words. No wonder that forty thousand Hindus—children, men and women, blind and lame, princes and peasants—climb thither every year and that five to six hundred of them yearly die there in happiness with the blessed name of God on their lips!

I paid my respects to some Mahatmas at Uttarkashi, and at Jamnotri and Kedarnath. On nearing Gangotri, I prayed to a living Mahatma about whom I had heard to bless me with his presence. He arrived five minutes before me, stark naked, with a beautiful body, a more beautiful face, and the most beautiful eyes. Saluting him, I offered him a cup of milk, and off he went, and disappeared among the hills.

Invited to a meal by a Swami, I refused to share it, for the Mahatma had become my guest and I could not eat before he did. After ten minutes he reappeared. I offered him the dish, which he accepted gladly and they gave me another. He asked me how long I intended to stay there, and I replied: "So long as your Holiness wishes." This answer pleased him. He spoke Hindi and was well versed in Sanskrit, and enjoyed hearing me repeat some of my Sanskrit hymns. At night he slept in a small room on hay, and I noticed that while other people were shivering with cold, he was profusely perspiring. He knew every niche of my mind, so I had

9. Shiva temple at Kedarnath (Photograph by Ashok Dilwali).

The Dream of the Himalayas

nothing to tell him, but allowed him to speak; it would have been an insult for me to explain what he already knew. His themes were spiritual. He had long loved me and had come for the sake of meeting me, and after five glorious days, he bid me continue my pilgrimage. I knelt before him for his blessing, and took leave of him with a heavy heart, but the encouragement derived from him obliterated all the hardships I had undergone, or which were to come on my way to Shri Badri Narayen, where Uddhava Swami, the disciple of Lord Shrikrishna, lives with the great sage Narada, the apostle of Devotion.

32

Who showed Me the Way?

SHRI BADRI NARAYEN has a manifold sanctity, for Nara, Narayan, Sanak, Sanandana, Sanatkumar, Shukacharya, Uddhava and many others practised penance there and attained the highest stage of yoga. The sacred river Alaknanda flows majestically at the bottom of the steps of the temple. There is a hot-water tank, where pilgrims take their sacred baths every morning and evening; in this very hot water I had not only to dip, but to remain long enough to recite from the Upanishads. The glacial torrents were so boisterous that I had to stand beside them and empty their water over me from my *kamandalu*. But though many succumb to these rigours, my Divine Master brought me through them all.

The dog, my faithful God-sent companion, still followed me. He had shared my meal on the first day, but after that shifted for himself and served me without demanding anything in return. The lower slopes of the Himalayas are clad in forests of tall trees, so dense that in places even noonday sun cannot pierce them. Their lofty dimness enfolded my meditations with awe. Birds' songs relieved the tedium of my travels, and towering peaks seemed to vie with one another. The path was so difficult that many a time a slip might have sent me rolling five thousand feet down into a torrent.

Avoiding the pilgrims' way, I chose the tracks used by the hillmen in order to meditate undisturbed; but last year's rains had in places so obliterated these that I had to crawl for yards together on hands and knees. We had to cross rivers by ice bridges and were drenched by torrential rains; hailstorms lashed us and blasts chapped our faces. The heat of the sun was at times unbearable; the water of the torrents became too cold for bathing; the long hours of pitch darkness in the gorges were terrible to endure, though lightning revealed momentary grandeurs; while the unintermitted roar of cascades and rapids deafened and stunned. When the ice melted, above the region of forests multitudes of flowers carpeted the high lawns with their varied brilliances of colour and intimacies of scent, to enchant the children of God who, leaving kith and kin, climb to worship Him among the peaks.

Nearing the crest of each ridge, I hoped to discover the desert prospect broken by some mountain village, but how rarely did my dream come true. The farms were few and far between, though the farmers were extremely devout and charitable. Poverty is a great virtue that fosters religious life. Poor men remember God more often than their richer brethren.

I found it advisable to obey the coolie in all that concerned his trade. One morning he told me that the sky threatened a heavy hailstorm, and since there was no shelter, not even a shrub's, on the way, we had better not risk our lives. I obeyed him, but there was a rich man, accompanied by a train of thirteen, who persisted in pressing forward. On the morrow, at the next village, the priest told us that those fourteen people had perished in the storm and not a bone of them was left, as they had been hurled into the ravine.

A man-eater in one region had taken a toll of nearly eight hundred pilgrims in seven years. Great hunts had not availed to kill him, so the Government ordered everyone to remain indoors between sunset and eight in the morning. My host there was a landowner, a government official, so I had to obey, though but for my obligations to him I should have run the risk.

The noon rest was necessary, but otherwise I preferred uninterrupted marches, though sometimes I became so tired I was forced to lie down and sing the Upanishads. The roaring Ganges allayed my thirst, and with tremendous music filled my heart with joy. Was it not the counterpart of that in the hearts of yogis?

I knelt down before the image of Shri Narayen in the temple and, with tears in my eyes, invoked His blessing, as the Sanskrit has it: "Salutations to Him, of supreme bliss, by whose grace the dumb speak and the lame climb mountains."

My faith in the many physicians who advised me not to attempt the Himalayas was considerable, but my fiath in Him had been far greater. I always thought: "Let Him who commands provide the possibility of fulfilment", and freedom from doubt proved to be protection from every danger.

My coolie became homesick. Having no money left to pay him, I wired to a friend at Bombay who sent a telegraphic money-order for twenty-five rupees, and we parted at Shrinagar. The man in charge of the monastery of Kali Kamliwale Bawa tried his best to get another coolie for me, but failed. The hanging bridge had been washed away and all communications with the next villages interrupted. I insisted on starting next day at noon, and left my carpet and blanket behind with him, not having the strength to carry them. I had not gone far when he caught me up with two small boys who offered to carry my luggage up to Rishikesh.

Determination to reach Vyasa Chatti on the Guru Pournima day, sacred to the sage Vyasa, the author of the great epic *Mahabharata* and of the division of the Vedas, made it a duty to bathe in the Vyasa Ganga before offering my evening prayers to Lord Dattatreya. There was scarcely the necessary time, but I was resolute. The boys could not keep pace with me. They said: "Swamiji, you go like the wind." Evening drew in with the town still far off. There was the Vyasa Ganga flowing down the hill. A prayer went up to sage Vyasa as I hurriedly searched for a footpath to the river. The sun was sinking fast. In nervous desperation I was about to dash down the hill to the river without finding the short cut; suddenly a hand was on my shoulder, and I encountered a loving glance while a gentle voice said: "What are you doing? See, here is the footpath!"

Having started forward in my haste, I then remembered that thanks were due to my benefactor, and looked back; no one was there. Realising who had helped me, with tears of gratitude in my eyes I ran down the path, threw off my clothes, tied the *koupin* round my loins and plunged into the river, had my bath, and then poured out oblations of water to my best-beloved Gurudeo, the Lord Dattatreya. Half the orange disk of the sun still rested on the horizon as I offered thanks for the close of that most blessed day on which my Lord had offered me a chance of worshipping Him. Copious tears were shed in gratitude for the trouble which He had undergone.

Two years later, at Poona, a Mahatma said to me: "Do you know who it was showed you the path that evening outside Vyasa

Who showed Me the Way?

Chatti?" I was astonished: how should he know of an incident concerning which my lips had never opened. He laughed and said: "The man who showed you the path was the sage Vyasa."

The leopard-like dog left me without taking leave as I was nearing Rishikesh on the return journey. My two little porters, who were by profession tailors and had frequently arrived at our night's resting-place three hours later than I did, as they could not keep up with me, came as far as the Kali Kamliwale Bawa monastery, where the good monks were delighted with them and with hearing from me how well they had served me; so they gave them plenty of wheat flour, lentils and potatoes for their journey home. I also gave them my umbrella, one blanket and one bed-sheet, and rather more money than we had agreed on, and the two cheerful little porters returned up the road thoroughly content.

My freinds welcomed me back to Rishikesh and nursed me, for not a pound of flesh remained on my bones, but slowly I recuperated, and then with many halts at length reached Bombay.

33

The Mandate

Having now travelled throughout India, sustained by my begging-bowl and my ideal, meeting all sorts of people, Englishmen, Parsis, Jains, Sikhs, Punjabis, Kashmerians, Bengalis, Mahrattas, the Southerners, Mohammedans, pariahs and courtesans, and partaken of their hospitality in order to understand their thoughts and offer my own in exchange when so desired. I could use both English and Hindi as well as my native Marathi and the learned Sanskrit, and had enough Gujrathi to get along with. The vast varieties of climate and food had tried me severely. In Punjab they eat wheat all the year round, in Madras Presidency, rice. Bengal, Maharashtra, Gujrath, Central India, Andhra, Malabar each has its own staple food and its own condiments. In the United Provinces more sugar, in Kashmere more salt, in Gujrath more ghee, in Andhra more chillies, in Madras more tamarind prevails. The Gujrathis boiled tea with spices; Punjabis add almonds, Kashmerians add salt; in Madras they like it as bitter as possible, and in the United Provinces they hardly drink it at all. The same with the oils used for cooking vegetables. The mode of serving, too, is different; on tables, on stools from one foot to three inches high, laid with brass, silver or bronze utensils, or with lotus, plaintain and other leaves. I had no preferences; whoever officiated for Him, God was always my host.

I waited for others to begin, so as to imitate them, for customs differ, and offence is given in diverse ways. So like a dead man, without initiative, without prejudice, taste or smell, everything in this world had become pure for me, and all belonged to Him who was the purest of the pure. My rules, therefore, permitted me neither to ask what would suit my health best nor to refuse what was offered. I kept silent, for whatever is given with love nourishes love. Many a sanyasin advised me to give up my vows or they would end by killing me, but I remained steadfast. What was killed was my personal fads and petty egoism, and that fond attachment I had felt for my body. I now lived for days or even weeks on dishes which I had disliked and refused, compensating them for the insults once hurled at them.

The confirmation of my faith was the reward of these years of trial. Intellectually I had before acquiesced in whatever the old sages had written about the comparative values of spirituality and worldliness, but experience, realisation, is another matter altogether. A man can talk about faith in God, sitting calmly in his easy chair, but when that faith is tested, he is likely to lose it. Face to face with the grim, savage nakedness of this world, with no wealth or friends but only God for refuge, then to find Him near is to find Him indeed. He had proved ever ready to bless me with a smile. That had been what I looked for, and that I had found. All honour and glory be His!

I purposely associated with the educated everywhere, for they were most able and ready to ridicule my faith. They thus tested its strength, and to have avoided them would have been to doubt. A learned friend of mine called me a barbarian for worshipping a stone: the footprints of Lord Dattatreya. I pleaded guilty, adding with the greatest emphasis I could command: "I will make that stone speak to me!" And has it not spoken? Both words and meaning were often difficult, but the blessed day came when I could lay my hands on my breast and say in public that, though I had been a turbulent child and at times obeyed with great reluctance, He had been with me and forgiven all my faults.

The crisis was fast approaching. My body ached continually; I hardly slept at night for groaning, and could not digest anything. My eyes refused to see, my ears refused to hear, my antrums were full of pus, my throat was sore, and my teeth shook in their sockets. I had eight attacks of influenza, and there was uric-acid trouble. Spleen and liver refused to work, the heart was very weak, and double hydrocele with symptoms of sarcoma prevented me from walking. There was pain in my knees, and my feet refused to carry the burden of my body any longer. My back had ached for well-nigh twenty-four years, and was become unendurable. My head was dizzy, and all my functions seemed bent on preparing me to welcome the worst. The thought of another life, with better opportunities for serving God, never left me.

The doctors were not reassuring. At last my master told me to let them operate for hydrocele Xantholesma, and I was admitted to the Free General Hospital at Bombay through the recommendation of an Indian doctor for whom I retain the greatest respect. As a pauper, I was left to myself, and was discharged after twenty-one days, only to go to another free hospital to be treated for other maladies. And when released, other doctor friends treated me with indigenous medicines during four months. Improvement came very slowly, my ailments left me one by one. I now built castles in the air: to remove to a small hut in the Himalayas on the banks of the Ganges, beg daily for bread, and constantly meditate on Him, until His will was that I should leave this body. I was sick of the world and its complexities. All traces of worldliness had left me.

But one day my master summoned me to his presence, and with affectionate glances asked me to sit down beside him. He rejoiced at the improvement in my health, and conversed on spiritual life, complimented me on my conduct, and in a mild tone said: "What if you went to England? A nice change for you, and you can at the same time see how your poems are appreciated by the English, and interpret the esoteric phase of Indian life to the West. Will that not be a fine mission!"

His words shocked me and received no reply. The matter rested there. As days passed, recollection of how the very Reverend Dr. R. Scott, Principal of the Wilson College, Bombay, in 1913 after my poems in English had been written, had asked me to visit England. He had been the first Englishman who was very keen about me and my poems; perhaps the time had come to fulfil his desire.

After a month my master again broached the subject, and I had to obey. But how go to England without a penny in my pocket? Would it not be best to make a preliminary tour through India and find whether there were any who cared sufficiently for my books and philosophy to finance me?

The Mandate

After two months' rest at Satara with a very dear friend, I started on my tour with the avowed object of going to Europe, prepared by a survey of the spiritual state of my own country, and backed by whatever financial help I might find.

34

Out at Last!

THE prophecy of the Kashmere astrologer was fulfilled, at last I was to serve mankind. Hitherto I had been occupied with my own situation, but now I had to think of mankind. My desire for solitude was overruled by the commands of my Divine Master.

Many ridiculed the idea of my going to the West. Why should I spend India's money in preaching to the English when Indians themselves refused to listen? The political future was all that interested them. Most educated Indians had very little faith in the spiritual culture of their country. I approached a rich, educated business man who had frequently reproached me for having no purpose in life, no ambition. When I told him of my mission, he shrugged his shoulders, and with a brazen face said: "Swamiji, why did you leave your Himalayas? This world is not for you. You will be disappointed. Better still, follow your old ways." Then, as though taking me into his confidence: "Please do not rely on mine or anybody else's help. Stand on your own legs!" Thanking him for his advice, I gave him my blessing and left him.

Political leaders, whom I consulted, wished me to preach to the masses. I replied that the masses were always ready to receive the message; now the educated had the greater need of it since they had lost their faith. This answer annoyed them, and I determined to visit the anglicised Indians. But first I appealed to the religious heads, in the strongholds of Hindu orthodoxy. Acharya of Shri Shringeri math, the head of all the monasteries of Shri Shankaracharya, was kind enough to give me permission to cross the ocean, and his blessing. Both the Acharyas of Shri Sankeshwar monastery gave their blessings and permission. The organiser of the Bharat Dharma Mahamandal gave me a general letter of introduction. The head of the Shri Vallabhacharya monastery at Nathdwara gave me his blessing. Some of the great Pandits thought mine a good idea, and that now was the psychological moment to realise it. They hoped it would bring about a right understanding between the East and the West. The late Maharajadhiraj of Darbhanga, who presided at the meeting of the Sanatanists, that is, the orthodox Hindus at Benares, gave me not only his consent but a few rupees for my expenses.

I went to Nepal in the north, and from there to Trivandrum and Madras in the south, trying to persuade representatives of every shade of religious opinion. Sometimes I succeeded, at others I failed miserably. "No foreign propaganda" was the watchword of the patriots with few exceptions. My mission was not a propaganda. I wished only to recount my experiences and hear that of others who strive to realise the divine, so as to note points of agreement rather than those of difference. Not to convince others, but to do his duty without regard to results, is the task of a monk. He is freed from caste, creed and religion, and lives in obedience to the supreme spirit only. All religions are the same to him, and he respects all prophets as various manifestations of the same spirit. He quarrels with no one, for he believes in the unity of life, the unity of faiths, the unity of prophets and the unity of Gods, no matter what names they may be known by.

Some of my friends said: "Why not win over the hearts of Englishmen here before going to England?" I accepted their advice, and was glad to find that the Agents to the Governor-General in Central India, Rajputana and Western India, after full enquiries, not only certified to my bona fides but gave me introductions to various States under their jurisdiction. Some were highly interested in my philosophy and extended their hospitality to me.

I gave no public lectures, wishing rather to convince an influential few than to stir crowds. I addressed many conversational meetings, and the discussion which followed was always sincere and heartfelt. I had my Sanskrit, Hindi and English writings with me, and I read them before appreciative audiences. They had slept for many years, but appealed to the devout. I met many Mahatmas, who all without exception applauded my motive and gave me their blessing. Great were the horror and dismay I felt at the widespread atmosphere of suspicion due to the political situation, which was most unpropitious to my efforts.

People had no time for philosophy and thought I was offering them a stone when they wanted bread. Some went so far as to suggest that I was a Government spy! Such nervousness could only excite my pity. Some of the best souls in India, though they were overworked with affairs, yet found time to listen to my message, and I must always feel proud to have found so much openness and consideration among them. My gratitude is due to Sir Prabha Shanker Pattani of Bhavnagar, His Highness the Maharaja Sahib Gaikwar of Baroda, Nawab Raza Nawaj Jung of Aurangabad Deccan, Mr. and Mrs. Hammabai, J.K. Mehta of Bombay and the Dowager Maharani Sahiba of Narsingarh of Central India. All honour to them, they and those like them are keeping ablaze the fire of spiritual life throughout the length and breadth of India.

35

The Assassin's Dagger

On my new quest I met the representatives of many religions. Some English missionaries took me into their confidence and told me that they did not understand the *Bible*; it was an Oriental book and they thought some Eastern sage should enlighten them on the teachings of the Lord Jesus. The East had given them a master, but they failed so to penetrate his secret as to follow him. An Indian finds nothing novel in Christianity, and one missionary was so sincere as to admit that bringing Christ's teachings to India was carrying snow to the Himalayas. He said Hindus are ready to worship the Lord Jesus, but most Christians were unwilling to believe in Lord Shrikrishna because they had dogmatic beliefs. Hindus believe in Lord Jesus as one of the prophets that come to this earth to preach the gospel of God, and believe that from time to time prophets come and will be coming till the end of the world. God incarnates in order to bless mankind with a message that answers to the aspirations of each age.

Every man stands spiritually alone and has his own ways of realising the divine. A wise man will not try to dissuade him from them, but will help him forward in them. Therein lies the true independence of thought and worship. To standardise divinity is like prescribing one medicine for all maladies. Every individual case must be treated on its merits, and a wise man will disinterestedly help each in every sincere effort.

At times, I failed very miserably to get into touch with those I met; few were willing to listen, and still fewer willing to attempt to realise the divine that they were conscious of. Yet unless we put into practice the beliefs we have, how are we to prove them or to discover better? Ignorance and egoism beget dogmatism, but realised divineness becomes part and parcel of a man's life.

The Autobiography of an Indian Monk

I was once more free as a bird. All the rules that hitherto bound me had been graciously remitted, and the only obligation laid upon me now was my mission. This often kept me so busy that I was compelled to rest, but as soon as I felt better, the work absorbed me once more. At Hyderabad, Deccan, I was warned that I should meet a hostile fanaticism, but this only made me the more zealous, for I hate no man and am willing to pay any price to dissolve hatred. Many a Mohammedan officer-of-state treated me very kindly; they had a broader outlook on life and did not share in the fury of the ignorant. Also Mohammedan fakirs conversed with me about the divine. Nor did we ever disagree; since both had realised God, there could be no division of opinion between us.

One day a fakir invited me to celebrate the anniversary of his father, who had been a great saint. A friendly Mohammedan officer took me to the place in his car, and whom should I see there but the Nawab Amin Jung Bahadur, the secretary to His Exalted Highness the Nizam, and very glad we were to meet again. He asked the singers to sing Hindi songs, as I was not acquainted with Urdu or Persian, and the evening was spent in praying to and praising God. We had supper together, and after some serene conversation on the top of a hill, the Nawab Sahib embraced me in the fullness of his heart, and left. By that time most of the people who had assembled there, to pray and dine, had departed, and only four remained while the fakir recited his poems, which I enjoyed listening to. The whole atmosphere was attuned to the clear twilight sky.

All of a sudden an Arab climbed to us with rolling eyes and smelling of liquor. He kissed the hands of the fakir and sat beside him, eyeing me very intently. The officer, suspecting danger, asked me to come down the hill to his car. The Arab got up and began to abuse me, accusing me of reviling the Prophet. I told him that I never did such things, and respected theirs as much as any prophet. He would not desist, but made a threatening move towards me. I rose, folded my hands and fronted him face to face, asserting that I had never reviled the Prophet, adding: "If you think in spite of my denial that you accuse me justly, I am ready to serve both you and your Prophet." His dagger flashed in the light, but God gave me sufficient strength to face it boldly. The fakir and the other gentlemen who were there stood aghast. They were helpless, for the Arab was too powerful for them. He scowled at me, and, nobody knows why, his expression changed suddenly and he recoiled and sheathed his dagger; then the fakir took him by the hand and told him that he was committing the gravest blunder against me, for no fault of mine. He was pacified. My friend, the officer, was still calling to me from his car down the hill and telling me in English to hurry up as there was danger, and I told the fakir that if the Arab was satisfied, I would descend the hill; then shook hands with them both and hurried to join my friend. He had grown nervous, foreseeing an ambush; and, by putting out the lights of the car all of a sudden, he thwarted two Arabs who were hidden near a bridge with the same intent as the one we had left.

Two days afterwards a Mohammedan friend of mine invited me for dinner and asked me how the Arab was induced to sheath his dagger. I told him, "The Arab knows that better than I." When we were having dinner, he asked me the same question; again I replied: "You know better than I." When we were about to part, he again asked me the very same question. I only said: "He alone knows", turning my eyes towards Heaven, and pointing upwards with my finger. My friend embraced me all of a sudden and looked at me with such keen, penetrating, loving eyes that I returned his embrace with an equal warmth, and we parted.

The effects on India of Western civilisation so far as her spiritual life is concerned are far from healthy. Not only in India, but the world over, the more spiritual life is neglected, the more inward misery is discovered. Civilisation's superstructure may be very fine indeed, but it totters like a house of cards, for the everlasting kingdom is established in men's hearts and not outwardly to dazzle their eyes.

The saints believe in the unity of life, the equality of souls, the beauty of harmlessness. They do not believe in fighting unless it be in defence of spiritual life. Every man is potentially divine. Human nature is full of frailties, but all the barriers of age, class, caste, creed, religion and country, fall before the conception of spiritual unity. Let the world listen to the ancient voice of love and enjoy happiness and peace!

36

I am Brahma!

I CAME to Bombay, and was glad to rejoin my master there and recount in detail all my experiences. He merely said: "His will be done!"

One day when I was sitting at his feet, he told me to carry on the work without fear or favour, for it was His work, and that men were only instruments which the divine hand played upon. He again laid stress on faith, and asked me to work and leave the result to God. After a while he looked at me with his beautiful eyes, beaming with confidence and ecstasy, and said: "Remember, I am Brahma, the supreme Spirit!" Those blessed words are still ringing in my ears, and will do so eternally.

I am Brahma is one of the four supreme sentences in the Vedas. The others are:

Thou art That, meaning Thou, O man, art the Eternal Brahma.
Verily Everything that Is, is Brahma.
The Supreme Wisdom is the Wisdom of the Brahma.

The most important questions that every man has to put to himself, are:

Who am I?
Who art Thou? and
What is this Universe?

And the Vedas, the most ancient scriptures in the world, have answered these questions in the above four sentences.

If you ask me: "If all is divine, how has evil originated? How can one man be more spiritual than another?" I reply: "Concepts that are true in material experience are no longer valid in the realm of spirit." Matter and spirit, illusion and reality, Maya and Brahma, are all equally eternal, and therefore the relations we indicate by the contrasted terms are inscrutable. Information cannot enlighten us concerning them; we can only realise something through experience. When a little girl grew to be eleven years of age, she said to her mother: "Why do you leave me at night and go to my father? What are you doing with him?" But her mother could only say: "When you are married, you will understand." No information can impart the essential on such matters. As a woman gives herself to her husband, when we concentrate, we apply our hearts to one thought to the exclusion of all others; we forgo the pleasures of the roving, unsettled mind and fasten on the essence of being, divine, unchangeable and ineffable, and of the joy that then grows up within us we can say nothing that the discursive intelligence can understand, save in distant images and parables, for language is sensuous and reflects the illusions of matter which forever veil and disguise the spirit.

But when the child in her turn is married, she will experience and realise what it was her mother could not tell her. So those who have not yet won joy through concentration will only realise that joy when they have.

On the 16th November 1930, I left Bombay by s.s. *Pilsna*, at 10 A.M. Before that I went to my master, knelt down before him, offered him flowers and fruits, and was offered my breakfast. He came to the stairs, shook hands with me, gave me his blessing, and with a loving glance bade me God-speed. I looked at him with imploring eyes, and saluting mentally again, descended the steps, mounted the car, and drove to the harbour.

A few friends were there to wish me *bon voyage*. I greeted them all, accepted their flowers and a few other offerings, and went abroad the ship. I was waving my orange handkerchief to them till at last we lost sight of each other.

Epilogue

I WAS in Paris. Over and above my other ailments I there caught influenza, and a distinguished lady "fell from the clouds", as she put it, and nursed me. Paris contained some who already had the habit of coming to consult me on spiritual questions. When my temperature stood at 105, she insisted that I must no longer see them, but I replied "Being kept here by the Grace of God, I must accept the tasks He sends my way, at no matter what cost." And I saw a gentleman who had called, and talked to him for two hours, after which she found my temperature had risen to 107. She did all she could for me, and at 10 P.M. that night left me to have her supper. I was coughing and groaning badly, and my suffering seemed to me unbearable. Suddenly my Master apeared in his physical form and stood at my bedside. I saluted Him mentally, and before I could rise He placed His hand on my breast, bent over me, gazed into my eyes with extreme affection, and vanished. Then I slept.

The next morning my temperature was normal. The nurse could scarcely believe her eyes. I was under the treatment of a French homoeopathic doctor, and after I was completely cured, I came to London on the 28th February, 1931.

Many a time I have been thus saved by my Master, and I must, in duty bound, say that my body and mind and soul belong to Him. He has conquered me through His love. Time and space cannot impede the will of my Master, nor can broken bones and raging fevers maintain themselves in contact with realised God. They are Maya, illusion; the soul can be freed from them.

I am a mendicant, a sanyasin: though belonging to the highest order of spirituality in India, my faith in God is all the power, wisdom and joy I have. But at the same time, let me say with all the

Epilogue

fervour that I can command, not even my faith in God can equal my faith in my Master who showed me the path and led me through various vicissitudes towards the light. Whatever of good is in me is due to Him, and if there is any evil He has no part in it. He, who was my friend when we were young, is my living God, my divine Self, my incarnate Brahma. Always shall I pray for His mercy and be proud to kneel down before Him, until this atom is lost in the One.

Prayer

Let us all protect one the other.
Let us all enjoy together.
Let us act valiantly together.
May spiritual knowledge ever shine before us.
Let us never hate one another.
And let Peace and Peace and Peace reign everywhere.

translated from the Vedas

GOD BLESS YOU!

Index

Abbott, Justin E. xxxvii
Abhang xxxvii
Achchabal 119
Adepts, the 79
adesh xxxiii, 76
Alaknanda 136
Agni-Stambhan 38
Ahasuerus xvi
'Ajapa-japa' xv
akasha 78
Akkasahib 4, 6, 7, 8, 10
Ambaji 54
America xxiii
Amraoti 1, 12, 14, 24, 32, 48, 59, 61, 62, 70, 83
Amritsar 115
An Indian Monk xxii, xxviii, xxix, xxxi, xxxii, xxxiii, xxxiv, xxxv, xxxvi, xxxvii
Anasooya 55
Andhra 140
Anglo-Indian 38
Anglo-Vernacular 15
Anna-Chhatram 114
Aphorisms of Yoga xxviii, xxix
Arab(s) 148, 149
Arabian Sea 129
Arjuna, Prince xxiii, 114
Aryan 118
Ashram, Tapovan 106
Asia xiii
Asiatic xviii, xx
At Thy Lotus-Feet 98
Athos Mount xiv, xv
Atma-Vidya 20
Atri 55, 110
Aurangabad, Nawab Raza Nawaj Jung of 146

Aurobindo xxii
Autobiography and Verses xxxvii
Autobiography of a Yogi xxxv
Avadhoota Geeta (Gita) xxix, 47
avatar 92
Ayodhya 125

Badnera xxiv, 1, 8, 12, 13, 99
Badrinath 109
Baghdad 41
Bahadur, Nawab Amin Jung 148
Bai, Bahina xxx, xxxvi, xxxvii
Bai, Godu 73
Bai, Janki 5
Balaji, Shri 129
Bannerjea, Professor 30
Baroda, Maharaja Sahib Gaikwar of 146
Belur monastery 127
Benares 10, 27, 55, 65, 125, 130; Hindus at 145
Bengal 140
Bengal, Bay of 129
Bengalis 140
Bernard, St. xv
Bhagwat 112
Bhakti Yoga. *See* yoga
Bhaoosahib 10, 17
Bharavi 41
Bhat 56
Bhatavdekar, Annasahib 73
Bhasha, Gouranda xxv
Bhavnagar, Sir Prabha Shankar Pattani of 146
Bhrigu, Sage xxiv, xxv
Bhuti 5
Bible, the 147
Bina 10, 17

Index

Blunt, Wilfred xiii
Bodhi tree 125
Bombay xxvii, xxviii, xxxiii, 36, 38, 43, 48, 51, 55, 56, 96, 101, 102, 127, 129, 130, 138, 139, 142, 150, 151; General Hospital 142
Botticelli xvi
Brahmacharya 75, 109
Brahma-deo 54, 55, 70, 113
Brahma xviii, xxix, xxxvi, 27, 30, 150, 151, 155; Eternal 150; Wisdom of the 150
Brahmin(s) 4, 5, 10, 13, 73
Brindavan 121
Bristowe, L.S. xxvii
Bruce, Curt xxiii
Buddha xviii, xxi, 125
Byzantine xiv, xvi

Cairo 41
Calcutta 126, 127
Calcutta University 32
California xxvii
Callistus xiv
Catholic xxi
celibacy 75
centuries, Christian xv
Chandrashekhar 98
charpai 59
Chatti, Vyasa 138
China xiii
Chinese xxi
Chitale, Mrs Mrinalini xxv, xxxiii
Christ, Lord Jesus xiv, xvi, xviii, 147
Christendom xvi
Christian xii, xiv, xx, 147
Christianity 147
Christabel xvi
civilization, Western 149
College, Bahuddin 50
College, Deccan xxiv
College, Morris xxiv, 23
College, Wilson 142
Comorin, Cape 129
courtesans, Indian xx

Dadar 44, 49

Dadasahib (Gujannan Purohit) 10, 11, 33, 36
dakshina 105
Dakshineshwar 127
Dal, Lake 117
Darbhanga, Maharajadhiraj of 145
Darwha 69; Mahatma of 71
Das, Durga xi
Dattatreya, Lord xv, xxv, xxix, xxxiii, 13, 20, 27, 36, 43, 44, 47, 48, 54, 55, 57, 58, 61, 64, 84, 85, 97, 102, 105, 109, 116, 113, 115, 121, 126, 127, 138, 141
Daman xxvi
Deccan 111
Delhi 113, 120
Devi-Bhagwata 12
Dharma, Bharat 144
dharmashala 114, 132
Dhavadshi 1
Dhola 50
Dilwali, Ashok 34
Doulatabad 127
Droupadi 12
Dwarka 109, 129, 130

Egyptian Legation xii
Ekadashi 87
Eliot, T.S. xxviii, xxix
Ellora 127
England xxvii, xxxiii, 27, 117, 142, 145
Englishman 111, 119
Englishmen 39, 41, 140, 145
English people 38
Europe xii, xiii, xxiii
European xiii, xvi, 74, 102; devotees xx; literature xii; music xvii; mystics xv
Excursion, the xvi

Faber xxviii
Fakir, Great 56
Family, the Hindu xxxiv
Foden, Mrs. Gwyneth xi, xxxi
French Rev. R.M. xiv
fulkas 132

Ganga-Dhama, Shiva 26

Index

Ganga, Vyasa 138
Ganges 9, 28, 65, 114, 115, 126, 130, 131, 137
Gangotri 131, 133
Ganguli, Mr. 25
Gaya 125
Gayatri mantra xv, 13, 36, 78
Geeta xxiii, xxviii, 12, 20, 31, 47, 68, 86, 92, 93, 100, 114
Gerber, William xxiii
Giri Order 44
Girnar, Mount xiv, xviii, xxi, xxv, xxvi, xxxv, 49, 51, 55, 61, 66, 74, 99, 102, 109, 110, 111
Gitanjali xii, xxxi
Gokul xxxvii, 121, 123
Gomukhi Kund 53
Gopees 121
Gorakhanath Hill 54
Greece xiii
Gregory, Lady xiv
Grihasta-Ashram 109
Gujrath 111, 140
Gujrathis 140
Guru-Charitra 18, 20, 31
gurudeo 85
Gurudeo, Shri 45

Hamsah, Soham xv
Hammabai, Mr. and Mrs. 146
Hanuman, Lord 20, 43
Harbinger of Love, The 97
Hardwar 114, 115
Hari xxxvii
Hatha-Yoga. *See* yoga
Hellas xvi
Himalayas xxxv, 44, 58, 112, 114, 117, 125, 130, 131, 136, 142, 144, 147; The Dream of the 129
Hindu 3, 4, 11; culture 73; philosophy 76; orthodoxy 147
Hindus, the 2, 74, 113, 125, 133, 147
Honey-Comb, The 98
Holy Krishna. *See* Krishna
Holy Mountain, The xxviii, xxxii
Hopkins, Gerard Manley xxxiii
Hubli 35

Hyderabad 80, 148

Ignatius xiv
In Quest of Myself 97
India xxiii, xxxiii, 44, 56, 92, 98, 109, 114; independence of xiii; Southern 129; Central 130, 140, 145, 146; Western 145
Indian Mysticism, London Institute of xxvii
Indian(s) xx, xxi, xxxi, 92, 111, 112, 144, 147
Indumati xxvi, 81

Jagadamba 24, 109
Jains 55, 140
Jala-Stambhan 38
James, Henry xii
Jammu 118
Janaka, King 89, 90
Japanese xxi
Jetalsar 50
Jesus, Lord. *See* Christ
Jhelum 117
Joshi, M.M. 50, 54, 86
Jumna xxxvii, 122, 123, 124, 131
Jumnotri 131, 133
Junagad 58, 59
Junnar 85

Kailash, Mount 44, 58
Kali 126
Kalyan 36
kamandalu 103, 104, 113, 119, 131, 136
Karma 1, 3, 12, 14, 19, 86
Karma Yoga. *See* yoga
Kanchi 129
Kashmere 115, 117, 140, 144; shawl 60, 64; rice pudding 119
Kashmerians 140
Kathiawar 111, 112, 129
Kedarnath, Shri xxvii, 131, 133
Kedgaon 43
Keertikar's building 44
Kolhapur 55
koupin 138

Index

Krishna, Lord. *See* Shrikrishna, Lord
Krishna, River xxxvi, 39, 128
Kubla Khan xvi
Kundalini, The 78, 80
Kurukshetra 114

Lahore 115, 119, 121
Lakes, Italian xv
Laxmibai, Queen 10
Lakshmi, Goddess 1, 2, 4, 20, 55
Lalamaharaj, Shri 69
Lancaster Gate, xxvii
Lawasha xxvi; Ashram at 106
Lonavala 97, 105
London xxii, xxiii, xxvii, 152

Macmillan xxviii, xxxii
Macmillan, Harold xxx
Madurai 129
Mahabharata 12, 89, 138
Mahalakshmi, Shri. *See* Lakshmi, Goddess
Mahamandal, Bharat Dharma xii
Maharaj, Shri Boa 59
Maharaj, Shri Narayen 43
Maharaja Shri Gajanan 60
Maharashtra xxx, 30, 49, 55, 90, 140
Mahatma(s) 3, 4, 8, 15, 16, 17, 26, 27, 28, 30, 31, 39, 40, 43
Mahratta 5, 20, 44, 80, 129, 140
Mahur, Mount xxv, xxxv, 55, 61, 62, 74
Majorca xxviii
Malabar 140
Maisahib 10
Mandal, Maharashtra 113
Mandodari 12
mantram, 'Ajapa-japa' xv
Marathi xxxiii, 14, 39, 63, 98
Marga-Sheersha 55
Marwar 16
Master, Divine 15, 18, 26, 35, 54
math, Kali Kamliwale Bawa's 115
math, Shri Shringeri, Acharya of 144
maths, Hindu xxvii
Mathura. *See* Muttra
Maya 151, 152
Mehta, J.K. (of Bombay) 146

Mi Ek Sanyasi xxxiii
Mirabai, Shri 121; Saint 126, 129
Mohammedan(s) xii, xiii, 148, 149
Mohammedan Fakir(s) 56, 148
Mohammedan 129
Mind of India, The xxiii
Mokashi-Punekar, S. xxix, 47
Monasteries 132, 138, 139
monastery, Shri Shankeshwar, Acharya of 144; Shri Vallabhacharya 145
monastery, St. Michael's xiv
monks, Christian xxxi; Indian xiii, xxxi
Moore, Thomas Struge xii, xiii, xxix, xxx
Moslems 56, 129
Mother, Divine 13
munj 13
Murree 119, 120
Museum and Library, Nehru Memorial xxix
Mussoorie 130, 131
Muttra (Mathura) 120, 121, 123, 124
Mystery, Mysticism is not 68
mystical classics, India's xxx

Nagpur xiv, 23, 24, 48
Nagnath, Shri 127
Naikins 35
N.A.L. xxxi
Narada 54, 135
Nara 136
Narayan, Shri Badri 131, 135, 136
Narayen, Shri 137
Nardhana 59, 60
Narsingarh, Dowager Maharani Sahiba of 146
Narsoba Wadi 34, 35, 37
Nasik 127, 130
Natekar, Shri xxv, 44
Nathdwara 145
Neminath 55
Nepal 145
New York xxiii
Nimbalker, Rao Rambha 80
Nivas, Prem xxvi, 106
Nizam, the late 80; His Exalted Highness 148

Index

Office, Holy xvi
Oriental 147
Oxford Book of Modern Verse xx

Pagan xiv
Pandit(s) 117, 119, 120, 145; Brahmin 118
Pandurang xxxvii
Pandvas 12
Papers, Purohit Swami xxiii, xxix
Paramahamsa, Ramakrishna Bhagwan 87, 126
Paris xxvii, 152
Parsis 140
Patanjali xxviii, xxxiii, 26, 36, 82, 90
Patiala 130
Pelham, Lady Elizabeth xi, xxvii
Persia xiii
philosophy, Vedantic xxx
pilgrim, Russian xiv
Pilgrim's Progress xxxi
pitri rin xxvi
Poona (Pune) xxiv, 23, 71, 73, 75, 80, 85, 98
Porebunder 130
Pournima, Guru 138
Pranayam 36
Pratyahara 38
Presidency, Madras 140
Protestant, Irish xiv
Provinces, United 140
Punjabis 140
Puri, Jagannath 109, 126
puris 109
puries 121, 122
Purohit, Gajannan xxiv
Purohit, Parvati xxv, xxvi
Purohit, Sadashiv 1
Puskaraj 113

Raiji's gardens 110
Raja-Yoga. *See* yoga
Rajkot 113
Rajputana 145
Ramachandra, Shri 12, 125
Ramatirtha xxii
Rameshwaram 109, 129
Random House xxiii

Ravana 12
Rawalpindi 120
Renaissance xvi, xxii
renunciation, Purohit Swami's xxix
Rishikesh 114, 115, 130, 131, 138, 139
rishis 133
Roy, Suresh Chandra 25
Royal, Astrologer 117, 119

saint, Irish xvi; Christian xxi
samadhi 88, 89
Sanak 136
Sanandana 136
Sandeepani, Sage 130
Sannyasa-Ashram 109
sanyasin 141, 152
sari 122
Satara 1, 86, 143
Saugor 18
Scott, Rev. Dr. R. 142
Sering-Pattam 129
Seva-Dharma 2
Shaila, Shri 127
Shankaracharya, Shri xxvi, 26, 109, 117; Monasteries of 144
Shirdi 85
Shiva, Lord xxvi, 4, 5, 16, 20, 43, 53, 54, 55, 99, 109, 127, 128, 129, 130
Shivaji, the Great 20, 129
Shrikrishna, Lord xxiii, xxxvi, 2, 12, 20, 47, 55, 87, 92, 100, 105, 112, 114, 120, 121-124, 147; infancy 129
Shrinagar 117, 119, 138
Shukacharya 89, 90, 136
Siddhartha, Prince xxv
Siddhasana 36, 79, 88
Sikh(s) 115, 140
Simeon xiv
Smith, Mrs. Rennie xi
Socrates 69
Somnath, Shri 129
Song of Silence, The 97
Songir 59
Southerners 140
Spenser, Edmund xvi
Stories of Indian Mysticism xxv
Sudama 130

Index

Sumati xxvi, 98
Swami, Eknath 20, 112
Swami, Gahininath 60
Swami, Hamsa (Natekar Swami) xxv, xxvi, xxviii, 42, 47
Swami, Janarden 127
Swami, Kartikeya 47
Swami, Natekar. *See* Swami, Hamsa
Swami, Purohit, life and Work of ⟩ xii, xxxvii
Swami, Ramdas xxxvi, 39
Swami, Santdeo 119
Swami, Siddharudha 35
Swami, Tembe 35
Swami, Uddhava 55, 112, 135, 136
Swami, Vivekananda xii, xxii, xxvii, 126

Tagore, Rabindranath xii, xxxi
Teertha, Kamandalu 104
Temple, Golden 115; Shri Ghrishneshwar 127; Kashi Vishvanath 125; Shiva 134
Ten Principal Upanishads, The xxiii, xxviii
theologian, Catholic xii
theologians, Byzantine xvi; mystical xiv
Tilak, Lokmanya xxvi, xxxii
Trimbakeshwar 130
Trinity, Lord of 58
Trivandrum 145
Tukaram, Sant xxxvi, xxxvii
Tukoba. *See* Tukaram
Tungarli Hills 105
Turner, Miss Vera xxvii

Ujjain 130
University, Bombay xxiv; Calcutta 32
Upanishad(s) xxiii, xxxiii, 13, 53, 93, 105, 111, 123, 136, 137; Sadguru 104, 108; translation of the xxviii
Uttarkashi 133

Vaijanath, Shri Parli 127
Vanaprastha 100, 109

Vasudeo 123
Vatican, the xxvii
Vedas 4, 8, 13, 64, 93, 111, 126, 129, 150, 154
veena 78
Valley, Tapti 59
Vidarbha xxiv
Viramgaon 50
Vishnu, Lord 54, 55
Visions and Beliefs xiv
Vivekananda, Swami xii, xxii, xxvii, 126
Voice From the Himalayas xxii
voyage, bon 151
Vyasa, Shri 89, 138, 139

Wai 56
Waste Land, The xxviii
Way of a Pilgrim, The xiv
westerners xxxiv
words and names, Indian xxxvii

Yeats, W.B., Nobel laureate xxii; Irish poet xxvii; Introduction to xxviii, xxix, xxx, xxxi, xxxii
Yeotmal 62
Yeats-Brown F. xxxi
yoga xxii; aphorisms of xxviii, 27, 82, 90; Bhakti 39, 97; greatness of 95; Hatha 36; Karma xxvii; path of 36; Raja 36; stage of 136; *Sutras* xxiii; truth of xxxv, 27; what is 100
Yogananda, Paramhansa xxxv
yogi xxix; Hindu xxxv; who practised meditation 26; powers xxxvi, 26, 38; worthy of a 45
Yogi, Master 55
yogic posture 27, 79
yogini 53
yogis 49; hearts of 137
Younghusband, Sir Francis xi, xxxi

Zhansi (Jhansi) 10, 13, 14
Zula, (Thula) Laxman 114, 131